"Gad Elbeheri is a powerhouse in the field of Dyslexia"
— Dr Gavin Reid, Psychologist and author.

T0347161

Motivating Students with Dyslexia

Bursting with concise and clear advice, in this book Gad Elbeheri explores why motivation for pupils with dyslexia can drop, and how this can be addressed before it impacts on learning.

Motivating Students with Dyslexia provides a variety of ideas for improving motivation, all one hundred tried and tested, and can be applied in the classroom immediately. With a focus on enhancing the skills and the self-sufficiency of teachers, this essential resource provides:

- An accessible summary of the theoretical groundings to motivation.
- A clear rationale of why particular strategies should be used.
- Advice on how to successfully plan, execute and evaluate learning at school and at home.

Ideal for teachers and SENCos around the world who are looking to improve or diversify motivation techniques for students with dyslexia, this book is a brilliant toolkit of inspiring ideas for increasing motivation among students with dyslexia at all levels of education.

Gad Elbeheri is Expert for the Centre for Child Evaluation & Teaching, Kuwait City, Kuwait.

Motivating Students with Dyslexia

100 Ideas for Empowering Teachers in the Classroom

Gad Elbeheri

Routledge
Taylor & Francis Group

LONDON AND NEW YORK

First edition published 2021
by Routledge
2 Park Square, Milton Park, Abingdon, Oxon OX14 4RN

and by Routledge
52 Vanderbilt Avenue, New York, NY 10017

Routledge is an imprint of the Taylor & Francis Group, an informa business

© 2021 Gad Elbeheri

British Library Cataloguing-in-Publication Data
A catalogue record for this book is available from the British Library

Library of Congress Cataloging-in-Publication Data
Names: Elbeheri, Gad, author.
Title: Motivating students with dyslexia : 100 ideas for
empowering teachers in the classroom / Gad Elbeheri.
Description: First edition. | Abingdon, Oxon ;
New York, NY : Routledge, [2021] |
Includes bibliographical references and index. |
Identifiers: LCCN 2020044569 (print) | LCCN 2020044570 (ebook) |
ISBN 9780367622374 (hardback) | ISBN 9780367622367 (paperback) |
ISBN 9781003108474 (ebook)
Subjects: LCSH: Dyslexics–Education. |
Motivation in education. | Effective teaching.
Classification: LCC LC4708 .E43 2021 (print) |
LCC LC4708 (ebook) | DDC 371.91/44–dc23
LC record available at https://lccn.loc.gov/2020044569
LC ebook record available at https://lccn.loc.gov/2020044570

ISBN: 978-0-367-62237-4 (hbk)
ISBN: 978-0-367-62236-7 (pbk)
ISBN: 978-1-003-10847-4 (ebk)

Typeset in Bembo
by Newgen Publishing UK

Contents

About the author

Gad Elbeheri is the Founder and Managing Director of Global Educational Consultants (Egypt). Previously, Dr. Elbeheri was a Dyslexia Country Expert for UNDP Kuwait, Dean of the Australian College of Kuwait and the Executive Director for the Centre for Child Evaluation & Teaching.

Dr. Elbeheri obtained his PhD from the University of Durham, UK and has a keen interest in cross-linguistic studies of Dyslexia, Learning Disabilities and Inclusion. Dr. Elbeheri has made over 40 conference and seminar presentations around the world. He has published over 50 different publications in English and Arabic in the field of dyslexia and its manifestations in Arabic. He has participated in producing nationally standardised tests, computer-based screening programmes, reports and documentaries.

"Ever since I was 10 years old, I have always been fascinated with how Motivation differs from one person to another and why do we actually lose it and how we can claim it back"

Introduction

What is it that motivates students to learn? Are they all aiming to please their parents or someone else or themselves? Are they after good grades and high achievements in life? Is it their desire to outperform their peers and their underlying drive to compete? Or is it their fear of failure? Is it their hope to generally succeed in life and feel welcomed and accepted in their community? Are they promised rewards to receive if they learn? Or does it simply make them happy to learn? What drives children to do things? Often, it's the prospect of succeeding or improving in something so as to succeed. The more children feel competent at a task, the more likely they are going to enjoy the activity and the more likely they want to get better at it. Success builds motivation which leads to more success. However, children with dyslexia typically experience more setbacks than their typically achieving counterparts[1]. They tend to face more challenges. Improvement and success for them may come more slowly or less frequently although they work equally hard or even harder sometimes to compensate for their dyslexia. This hampers their motivation.

Researchers with different backgrounds in education, psychology, sociology, economics and politics have all been trying to fully understand and comprehend motivation so that they can maximise the outcomes of the learning process or increase the work production of their employees which will eventually improve the overall efficiency of the educational or employment systems[2]. Although they differ in the way they approach the study of motivation, the tools they employ to measure it and the methods they utilise to collect their data and analyse it and finally the underpinning principles tend to be very similar[3].

What practices can we employ to increase the motivation of individuals in our society? What should we do as parents, educators, work managers or politicians to increase the participation, engagement, work productivity, study times and the overall motivation of our target audience? This book aims to answer this simple question albeit in the field of education and in the case of students with dyslexia. What can teachers do at school to increase the motivation of their students with dyslexia to learn[4]? What is the required understanding they must have to help them do so? What are the tools they should employ to tackle this task? What practical and quick strategies can they employ today to assist them in such a quest?

I believe that enabling and empowering teachers by understanding motivation would manifest itself during the various stages of the learning experience; i.e., while teachers are planning for learning, while they are engaging in teaching and instruction, and finally while they are reflecting, assessing and evaluating the learning outcomes[5]. Effective learning in and outside the classroom depends to a great extent on teachers' abilities to maintain the interest that initially brought their students to the classroom in the first place and the interest of those students to engage in the various learning activities they seek to make available to them[6].

The current book is made up of two Parts. Part I sets the scene for Part II and starts with the definition of dyslexia and its symptoms before proceeding to focus on the issue of motivation. It clarifies the types of motivation according to its original source and destination and also explains the underlying process of motivation and the various theories proposed to explain it. Part I is essential because as a teacher who wants to motivate your students with dyslexia in the classroom, you need to understand motivation yourself first[7]. No one expects you to be able to motivate someone else if you do not know what motivation is, or if you do not know how many types of motivation there are or why some of your students are motivated while others are not? Part I of this book answers all those questions, so it is very important that you read it carefully and make your own notes and observations regarding motivation. The contents of Part I of the book is relevant to all teachers and not only those who teach students with dyslexia. Anyone interested in motivating themselves or others around them will benefit from Part I of this book.

Part II of this book contains ideas and strategies which focuses on 'how to do it'. Ideas listed in Part II are essential to teachers both inside and outside of the classroom. The ideas in Part II are listed according to the following four basic categories:

1 Motivate your students with dyslexia after you understand motivation yourself.

2 Motivate your students with dyslexia by developing your own personal qualities as a teacher.

3 Motivate your students with dyslexia by improving your understanding of the learning process.

4 Motivate your students with dyslexia by acquiring specific techniques to apply inside and outside the classroom.

The 100 ideas contained in Part II of the book will be listed under those general headings to make it easier for the reader to use and reference. You can also focus on the ones you are not familiar with or review the ones you are familiar with using those headings. In general, as a teacher of students with dyslexia, you need to know and utilise many of those ideas on a daily basis and try to find out which ones work with which students and adjust accordingly[8]. I wrote the book for teachers using an accessible simple language. I tried to avoid technical jargon. I also placed the references as footnotes so as not to disrupt the flow of ideas. Enjoy reading the book and if I have missed any other ideas that you think I should include in my future editions, kindly write and advise me.

Gad Elbeheri,
Cairo, 2020

Notes

1 McLean, 2004.
2 Barry, 2007.
3 Broussard & Garrison, 2004.
4 Dörnyei, 2011.
5 Usher & Kober, 2012.
6 Pintirch, 2003.
7 Stipek, 2002.
8 Dörnyei & Ushioda 2013.

Part I

Dyslexia and motivation

1 Dyslexia

Definition[1]

Below I list three definitions of dyslexia: The first proposed by the International Dyslexia Association in the US, the second by the British Dyslexia Association (its British counterpart) and the third by the World Health Organisation. Although there are more definitions that I can list (such as the definitions proposed by the American Psychiatric Association, the World Federation of Neurologists or by the British Psychological Society), I choose not to as my intention is to only give teachers a context for dyslexia and its signs so that I can proceed to focus on how to motivate students with dyslexia to learn which is the aim of this book[2]. Regardless of which definition you adopt; it is important that you seek to help your students with dyslexia to achieve their full potential.

International Dyslexia Association

The International Dyslexia Association (IDA) is a non-profit organisation based in Baltimore, Maryland, USA. It is considered the oldest and biggest non-profit dyslexia organisation in the world. On 12 November 2002, the IDA's Board of Directors endorsed the following dyslexia definition:

Dyslexia is a specific learning disability that is neurobiological in origin. It is characterised by difficulties with accurate and/or fluent word recognition and by poor spelling and decoding abilities. These difficulties typically result from a deficit in the phonological component of language that is often unexpected in relation to other cognitive abilities and the provision of effective classroom instruction. Secondary consequences may include problems in reading comprehension and reduced reading experience that can impede growth of vocabulary and background knowledge[3].

British Dyslexia Association

British Dyslexia Association

The British Dyslexia Association (BDA) is one of the oldest non-profit dyslexia association in the UK. The BDA has adopted the following definition of dyslexia:

> Dyslexia is a learning difficulty that primarily affects the skills involved in accurate and fluent word reading and spelling. Characteristic features of dyslexia are difficulties in phonological awareness, verbal memory and verbal processing speed. Dyslexia occurs across the range of intellectual abilities. It is best thought of as a continuum, not a distinct category, and there are no clear cut-off points. Co-occurring difficulties may be seen in aspects of language, motor co-ordination, mental calculation, concentration and personal organisation, but these are not, by themselves, markers of dyslexia. A good indication of the severity and persistence of dyslexic difficulties can be gained by examining how the individual responds or has responded to well-founded intervention.
>
> In addition to these characteristics, the BDA acknowledges the visual and auditory processing difficulties that some individuals with dyslexia can experience and points out that dyslexic readers can show a combination of abilities and difficulties that affect the learning process. Some also have strengths in other areas, such as design, problem solving, creative skills, interactive skills and oral skills[4].

World Health Organization

The World Health Organization (WHO) produces its own International Statistical Classification of Diseases and Related Health Problems which is known for short as ICD. ICD-10 is the 10th revision of it and it was published in 1992. ICD-10 listed the following definition of dyslexia:

> Dyslexia, also known as reading disorder, is characterised by trouble with reading despite normal intelligence. Different people are affected to varying degrees. Problems may include difficulties in spelling words, reading quickly, writing words, 'sounding out' words in the head, pronouncing words when reading aloud and understanding what one reads. Often these difficulties are first noticed at school. The difficulties are involuntary and people with this disorder have a normal desire to learn[5].

This is a follow up operational definition of dyslexia in 1993 by the same organisation:

A score on reading accuracy and/or comprehension that is at least 2 standard errors of prediction below the level expected on the basis of the child's chronological age and general intelligence, with both reading skills and IQ assessed in an individually administered test standardised for the child's culture and educational system[6].

As you can see from the listed definitions above, dyslexia is a very well documented field of study which attracts researchers from different diverse fields such as educators, policy makers, psychologists, speech and language therapists, and medical professionals. It enjoys the attention of all such multidisciplinary teams of interested professionals who in essence are interested in finding out how students read generally and how students with dyslexia can be supported.

Notes

1 The focus of this book is on developmental dyslexia not acquired dyslexia.
2 American Psychiatric Association, 2013.
3 The International Dyslexia Association, https://dyslexiaida.org/definition-of-dyslexia.
4 The British Dyslexia Association, www.bdadyslexia.org.uk/dyslexia/about-dyslexia/what-is-dyslexia.
5 The International Classifications of Diseases, https://icd.codes/icd10cm/F810.
6 Smythe et al., 2004.

The signs for dyslexia are numerous and they depend on the age of the individual, i.e., before starting school as opposed to early years or primary school and even adults. Both the International Dyslexia Association and the British Dyslexia Association have excellent resources on their websites regarding signs of dyslexia that you can consult and download. For now, it is important for you as a teacher to realise that dyslexia may manifest itself in the following ways: Learning to speak, learning letters and their sounds, organising written and spoken language, memorising number facts, reading speed, spelling, learning comprehension and learning a foreign language. If you are looking for age specific signs of dyslexia, consult the websites of both organisations for detailed symptoms. However, note that not all students with dyslexia will have all of the mentioned difficulties. As a teacher, you might have access to a dyslexia checklist or you may even apply open tests designed for teachers, but you cannot formally diagnose dyslexia as this process requires a full psycho-educational evaluation and a technical report which is usually performed by a qualified and registered educational psychologist.

Motivation is derived from the Greek word 'movere' which literally means to move. Motivation in simple terms is therefore the movement towards the aim that we pursue. It concerns itself with the magnitude and the direction of our human behaviour[1]. Everything in our universe moves. We as human beings living on earth have therefore acquired our movement by default from our moving earth. The state of movement and motivation is our natural state of being; i.e., our default state of being. Being unmotivated sometimes and losing our motivation and experiencing loss and in extreme cases depression is therefore the exception to the norm. Motivation involves the choice of a particular action; the persistence with it and the effort expended on it. It is our internal state that serves to activate and energise our behaviour and gives it direction. When an individual is motivated, he feels energised to act, whereas an unmotivated person feels no impetus to do so[2]. Different people have different amounts of motivation. Human motivation can vary not only in level and intensity, but also in orientation and type (Shape 1).

Shape 1 Motivation.

Motivation summary

- We are all motivated by nature (motivation is our default state).
- Not being motivated is therefore 'an exception'.
- We lose motivation when we lose our aim.
- Aim is first lost then low energy follows.
- As a teacher, focus on your search for reasons why your students lost their aim.
- Once you identify reasons for losing the aim, you can guide your students in their journey to claim back their natural state of being.

Notes

1 Dörnyei & Ushioda, 2013.
2 Ryan & Deci, 2000a.

If motivation is movement towards the goal we identified as the aim we seek, and if our universe is in a constant state of movement, and if we are merely objects in space, then surely physics as a field of study can help us utilise the natural physical laws that govern movements of objects in space. Therefore, I am proposing that we utilise the Laws of Motion to explain what motivation is and how it works.

First Law of Motion:

Every object persists in its state of rest or uniform motion in a straight line, unless it is compelled to change that state by forces impressed on it[2].

If we substitute the word 'object' by the word 'student with dyslexia', the law will apply. We as humans are also objects in space. So, we move according to the force applied on us. Such a force can be internal (intrinsic) or external (extrinsic) which will be explained below. Internal forces are explained by many theories most famous of them all is Maslow's Hierarchy of Needs. External forces are imposed upon us by our society, community, parenting, systems and values around us. The four dimensions of such external motivating forces are explained below in detail.

Types of motivation according to the origins of the force

Intrinsic motivation[3]

To be intrinsically motivated means to execute a task or perform an activity because of an inherent satisfaction arising from it rather than due to some separate outcome[4].

To be extrinsically motivated means to execute a task or perform an activity to attain some separable outcome.

There are four dimensions to extrinsic motivation[5]:

1   External regulation: Individual focuses on rewards or punishments resulting from the activity.
2   Introjection: Activity is undertaken to secure approval from others.
3   Identification: Individual begins, consciously, to value the activity.
4   Integration: Outcomes of the activity are congruous with the individual's goals.

The First Law of Motion above talks of forces that are applied on objects. Given that students with dyslexia are objects in space, what are those forces that are applied on them? The answer is simple and has been explained differently by different researchers; i.e., the most famous one of them in my opinion is Maslow's Hierarchy of Needs Theory. Full account of various theories will be given under that heading later on in this part of the book. For now, the forces applied on those students are their needs. They cannot live without the need to eat and drink, and sleep and rest. Once these are satisfied, according to Maslow, then comes the need to feel secure and happy and be loved and belong. Once those are met, then comes the need to respect themselves and others and to learn and grow and eventually the need to self-actualise.

Second Law of Motion:

The acceleration of an object as produced by a net force is directly proportional to the magnitude of the net force, in the same direction as the net force, and inversely proportional to the mass of the object[6].

This is a very important part regarding the nature of motivation. The more the force applied on us to act and move (whether internal or external) the more we move. This is what really makes a difference from a 'highly driven' person and a not so highly driven one; between those who are extremely motivated and want to work non-stop to achieve their ambition and those who are less so. It is the force applied on them (note that they themselves can also apply such force upon themselves in which case we call this internal motivation or internal drive)[7].

Types of motivation according to the destination of the force

Positive motivation:

Refers to the joy or optimism one feels when the task is completed.

Negative motivation:

Refers to the undesirable outcomes one feels when the task is not completed.

Notes

1 Guay et al., 2010.
2 NASA, www.grc.nasa.gov.
3 Wilson, 2011.
4 Weiner, 1979.
5 Ryan & Deci, 2000b.
6 The Physics Classroom, www.physicsclassroom.com/class/newtlaws.
7 Chan, 1994.

5 Motivation
Theories[1]

In order to motivate students, their attitudes and behaviours must be first understood. Such an understanding, i.e., motivation theories, can provide us with the necessary background information concerning the multifaceted aspects of motivation as a psychological process. Below is a brief overview of the theories of motivation[2].

Hierarchy of needs theory

I think as a teacher, you should be very familiar with Maslow's Hierarchy of Needs theory. It is well a well-known theory that has excellent applications in the educational field. Maslow's famous pyramid like shape includes five levels and one must satisfy or fulfil needs on the lower levels of the pyramid before moving up to higher levels. Five levels that Maslow identified are:

1. Physiological needs,
2. Safety needs,
3. Social needs,
4. Esteem needs, and
5. Self-actualisation needs.

Physiological needs are proposed to include air, food, water and shelter. Safety needs on the other hand are the need to feel safe and protected against danger and harm. Social needs include having the sense of belonging and of being loved. Esteem needs include having attention, confidence, freedom, independence, recognition and self-respect. Finally,

Self-actualisation is a process of one coming to terms with one's fullest potential.

Students whose physiological needs are not being met inside the classroom may not be motivated to learn and may find it difficult to benefit from the instructional opportunities teachers are working hard to make available. Hungry students are rarely motivated to learn or pay attention if all they think about is food. The same is true for thirsty students or those wanting to go to the bathroom. Similarly, students in hot classrooms, or those who are feeling cold, might also be affected as again their physiological needs are not being met. Accordingly, the child is most likely be motivated to achieve their physiological needs first before proceeding to fulfilling their other needs that are related to classroom learning.

Students with dyslexia are no exception to this rule and should have their physiological needs as well as their social needs met before being considered to have low motivation to learn. If those basic needs are not being met, it will no doubt negatively affect their motivation for learning. Students who have just transferred schools and have not made friends yet, or those who are not being accepted by their peers at school yet, may experience a loss of motivation because of their feelings of isolation. The same applies to threatened students, or those whose self-esteem is very low. Feeling independent, recognised and appreciated have an important influence on motivation, whereas feeling helpless, unappreciated and ignored are likely to hamper motivation.

Reinforcement theory

This theory describes two types of reinforcement: Positive and negative reinforcers and it views motivation as a continuous process of reinforcement. For example, if a teacher wishes for one of their students to pay more attention, then this can be achieved by:

1 Frowning which is a negative reinforcement in this case if the student does not pay attention, or
2 Encouraging the student to pay more attention with a promise of a social reward later which is a positive reinforcement, or
3 Simply cancelling that student's break time which is a punishment in this case.

All teachers know that reinforcement is needed and necessary for learning and this theory highlights how important this process is. Although there is disagreement regarding which type of reinforcement is better, i.e., negative versus positive, almost all agree that reinforcement is necessary for learning and for the repetition of the required behaviour.

Need for achievement theory

McClelland[3] identified three motivators that he believed we all have:

1   A need for achievement,
2   A need for affiliation, and
3   A need for power.

People will have different characteristics depending on their dominant motivator. This theory focuses on students with an increased level of need for achievement which leads to an increased level of self-esteem. According to this theory, students with a high level of need for achievement are always seeking ways to achieve new successes regardless of their surroundings. If a need is powerful enough within an individual, it can positively affect the intrinsic motivation of that individual to demonstrate behaviour which leads to satisfaction on accomplishing the need. According to this theory, those motivators are learned. Regardless of our gender, culture or age, we all have three motivating drivers, though one of those drivers will be dominant. This dominant motivator depends largely on our culture and life experiences.

Locus of control theory

Locus of control is the degree to which students believe they have control over the results of events in their own lives, as opposed to external forces that lie beyond their control. According to this theory, students' locus of control is either internal or external. Students who have an internal locus of control believe that they can control their own life while people who have an external locus of control believe that their decisions and life are controlled by environmental factors which they cannot influence, or that chance or fate controls their lives. Students with a strong internal locus of control believe events in their life derive primarily from their own actions. Students with more of an internal locus of control, when receiving exam results, tend to praise or blame themselves and their abilities. Students with a strong external locus of control tend to praise or blame external factors such as the teacher or the level of difficulty of the exam itself. An important consequent aspect of control theory is self-regulation. Students are seen as intelligent, goal-driven individuals who control their activities in order to achieve their objectives, goals and needs. Accordingly, teachers should give students with dyslexia things to control and help them control the things in their learning path. Teachers should not try to control everything in the learning environment, instead they should see the world as a series of choices that their students would have to make.

Self determination theory

According to self determination theory[4], there are three basic human psychological needs:

1 Autonomy,
2 Relatedness, and
3 Competence.

When these psychological human needs are satisfied, they enhance autonomous motivation which will in turn result in autonomous internalisation of behaviours that have been otherwise extrinsic in origin. The environment plays a significant part through the satisfaction process for those three basic psychological needs. This theory assigns significant roles to other players in the academic life of the learner, i.e., parents, teachers and peers[5].

Expectancy theory

Vroom's (1964) theory of motivation is based on the following three elements:

1 Expectancy: Which is the belief that a student's effort will result in the attainment of desired performance goals;
2 Instrumentality: Which is the belief that a student will receive a reward if the performance expectation is met (either intrinsic or extrinsic); and
3 Valence: Which is the value the student places on the rewards based on their needs, goals, values and sources of motivation.

If a task presented to a learner can be achieved, this fulfils the expectancy criterion. It means that there must be something in it for the learner who must feel that it will benefit him. This links with the 'valence' criterion which indicates that the learner must value the reward or the outcome of completing the task. Therefore, it is important to start with the learner's needs and interests. There is little point in suggesting a reward that is of little interest or value to the learner.

No one theory can comprehensively explain motivation[6]. Not only is motivation research in essence trying to deconstruct why humans act and think the way they do on an individual level, but social factors play their part in how and why we relate and react to things, too[7]. Understandably, all this makes motivation an enormously complex construct, but nevertheless a most important one. Regardless of the theory you find appealing to you as a teacher, they all have educational implications and they should all help you figure out how best to support your students with dyslexia in the classroom. You will find that in certain situations, different theories explain different motivational tendencies among students with dyslexia and that is why it is important that you as a teacher reflect on the various motivational theories.

Notes

1   Graham & Weiner, 1996.
2   National Research Council, 2004.
3   McClelland, 2001.
4   Deci & Ryan, 1985.
5   Rigby et al., 1992.
6   Dörnyei, 2011.
7   Dörnyei, 2003.

6 Motivation

Sources

Listed below are different sources of motivation that have been studied[1].

Behavioural/ External	• Elicited by stimulus connected to innately connected stimulus. • Obtain desired and pleasant consequences (rewards) or escape undesired, unpleasant consequences.
Social	• Imitaste positive models. • Acquire social competence skills. • Be part of a group or a community.
Biological	• Increase/decrease stimulation. • Activate senses. • Decrease hunger, thirst, discomfort. • Maintain balance.
Cognitive	• Maintain attention to something interesting or threatening. • Develop meaning or understanding. • Solve a problem or make a decision. • Eliminate threat or risk.
Affective	• Increase feeling good. • Decrease feeling bad. • Increase security or decrease threats. • Maintain optimism and enthusiasm.
Conative	Meet individually developed goals. Obtain personal dream. Take control of one's life. Reduce other's control of one's life.
Spiritual	Understand purpose of one's life.

Note

1 Huitt, 2011.

Part II

100 ideas to motivate students with dyslexia

Now that you have been provided with a brief introduction on dyslexia and motivation, I move to the second part of the book. In this part, the focus is on the ideas prepared for you so that you can apply them at school. Those ideas should assist you in boosting the motivation of your students with dyslexia.'It's been said that motivation doesn't last.Well, neither does bathing.That's why we recommend it daily'. This is, although funny, very true and captures what I would like to do in this part of the book. I recommend that you familiarise yourself with the ideas listed in this part and perhaps use those ideas regularly.You may even consider trying a new idea a day. Some teachers will be quite comfortable with many of the ideas presented if they have not already used them regularly before in their daily teaching. Other ideas may be novel and will sound interesting for some. Not every single idea will work with every child with dyslexia.You have to observe and decide for yourself which of those ideas work with your student with dyslexia and which ones do not.There is not a single way to motivate your student because they are all different and respond differently to those ideas depending on the current circumstances that they are in at the moment. To make your search easier and faster, I divided them into four major sections as follows:

1. Ideas based on your own understanding of motivation, i.e., if you understand motivation fully then you already possess some knowledge on how to motivate your students.
2. Ideas based on your own personal qualities as a teacher. Good teachers should have those excellent and motivating qualities and if you would like to motivate your students with dyslexia, focus on developing those qualities in yourself.

3   Ideas based on your own understanding of the learning process itself, such as theories of learning, principles of learning, conditions of learning and assessment of and for learning.

4   Ideas based on some recommended specific techniques for teachers to do to boost the motivation of their students.

Understand how motivation works

Having read the first part of the book, I am hopeful that you now appreciate that motivation is a skill many students need to learn. Students need to learn both:

1 How to get motivated; and
2 How to stay motivated.

Explain motivation to your students and use simple accessible language and illustrate it. Explain the different types of motivation to them and try and explain the actual process because this will help them find their lost motivation. Engage your students and work with them on figuring out what keeps them on task, and what does not. Draw a circle and divide it into two and write intrinsic in one side and extrinsic in the other and ask them to give you examples of each that they can identify within their local surroundings at school. This will no doubt take some effort from you at the beginning, but find what works for your students. As a teacher, it is always useful to keep in mind that what motivates you or some of your students with dyslexia may not work for your other students or for your teenager students. Different people are motivated differently and to a different degree and it is very important that your students with dyslexia understand that and understand what they need to do in order to accelerate and increase their motivation when they feel it is slowing down.

Motivation energises behaviour and keeps it sustained and focused over longer periods of time. Explaining this fact early on to students with dyslexia increases their own metacognition and awareness of motivation and assists them in self reflecting, which in turn increases their motivation and on task behaviour. Provide them with plenty of examples regarding intrinsic and extrinsic motivation and ask them for their type. Provide them with examples of what you do as a teacher when you would like to keep yourself motivated and ask them if they have similar tips for their fellow students in the class that they can share. You can always ask your students to prepare a presentation about motivation and present it to the whole class or even act out a short play about a motivated student who lost his motivation and someone is trying to help them get it back. Make the word motivation and the meaning behind it understood, repeated and accepted in your students' everyday vocabulary. It is what will keep them on task and what will provide them with the support needed to finish the tasks and assignments at hand.

Create a safe learning environment

Learning does not take place when you feel threatened. When students with dyslexia feel threatened, most of their focus will be on how to remove such threats. Alternatively, they may be consumed by fears which feeds their anxiety. Teachers should work hard to ensure that students with dyslexia know for sure that it is safe to ask for help. Students with dyslexia learn best and are more likely to ask for help in the classroom when a culture of learning is promoted and when mistakes are welcomed and considered a natural component of the learning process. Learning inside the classroom and at home must not merely focus on performance and competition[1]. It is always good practice to allow students and encourage them to ask their own classmates and peers for assistance. Peers can be an excellent source for learning in addition to teachers. Peers' role is vital in promoting the learning process inside the classroom if it is executed professionally and away from aspects of 'cheating' and the fear that always accompanies it. Students with dyslexia who are engaged in peer assistance whether they are the ones asking for the help or the ones providing it benefit from such a culture of peer assistance inside the classroom.

   Spend time and effort at the beginning of the school year to structure a process where peer assistance is encouraged and supported to avoid cheating and the fear that comes with it. The benefits of peer help and support and the process of how to seek it and what is acceptable and what is not and what to say and when are you allowed to engage in such peer assistance are all aspects that can be explained and initiated by teachers right at the beginning in order to structure such a useful process. Peer assistance and support is an element that helps in ensuring a safe and supporting environment for learning is maintained. Students with dyslexia tend to fulfil the expectations of what the adults around them communicate and hold for them. Motivate your students with dyslexia by focusing on what they can do rather than focusing on what they are not allowed to. Fear is not an effective motivator. Do you think that students with dyslexia who worry about the anger of their teachers and parents will eventually thrive? Students who experience fear for prolonged periods of time are more likely to become anxious students. Some students with dyslexia may develop test anxiety due to their excessive fear of letting someone down or performing badly in a task or obtaining a bad grade. Make your classroom a positive place by being supportive, positive and enthusiastic. Ensure your classroom is safe and that your student feels comfortable to ask questions and above all to ask for help when they need it.

Give learners autonomy

Autonomy is our ability to be responsible for our own affairs. Learners' autonomy is a learner's ability to take control of their own learning. Becoming an autonomous learner is very beneficial for the learner themselves and the learning process. Developing learner autonomy involves learning how to learn and is a gradual process. Learners may find themselves in situations where they do not get the support of their parents nor their teachers and therefore becoming autonomous learners enable them to depend on themselves in such instances. Autonomous learners are therefore likely to be more efficient in their own learning since their learning will be more personal and focused. The same skills autonomous learners need in the learning environment will also support them in the future notably in the workplace.

Parents and teachers have an important role to play in developing learner autonomy. The learning environment needs to provide opportunities for the learner to take control of their own learning. This may include opportunities for peer and self-assessment or performing activities with students after negotiating them first. Learners will initially lack the ability to identify goals or plan their learning. Teachers and parents can support them by scaffolding the learning process. They can also help by suggesting suitable goals or negotiating an agreed upon timetable. Students with dyslexia can also be given autonomy in choosing which reading texts to read and which subtopics to choose from and which method of expressing learning they are most comfortable with[2]. They can also be given the choice to submit assignments once completed or allowing them to mark their own papers or even scoring their own grades. Allowing students to monitor their own progress over time develops their autonomy. Regardless of the techniques used to develop learners' autonomy, it is important not to remove the help and the support system too quickly as this can in fact demotivate learners.

In order to become autonomous, learners need to be exposed to a range of useful learning activities and have the opportunity to evaluate and reflect on them. This will be achieved by a combination of efforts by the teacher, peers and the student. Working with others in this way can be difficult for some students with dyslexia, who may not be used to viewing learning as a social activity, and the autonomous learner therefore needs to develop social skills such as empathy, tolerance and understanding of difference, as well as the ability to explain, discuss and negotiate with the teacher and other learners. In short, developing learner autonomy means developing a wide range of academic, intellectual, personal and interpersonal skills, requiring engagement with cognitive, metacognitive, affective and social dimensions.

Give learners choice

Giving your students with dyslexia a choice in how they are learning and what materials are being used to learn or even the pace of their learning is a powerful tool for transforming your classrooms. Giving your students a choice is effective, cost free, takes little time to prepare and has a high impact on your students' engagement. Some teachers feel uneasy about giving their students with dyslexia control over the learning situation, but giving students the power of choice in the classroom does not mean that a classroom turns into chaos or becomes unruly. You can always achieve this gradually to allow your students to become more active in their learning process. Once this is established, it will free up more of your time as a teacher to focus on facilitating learning and guiding the learning process instead of focusing on mere instructions all the time. When teachers make the shift towards giving their students more ownership of their learning, it tends to pay off in student motivation and engagement. Choices that promote student control, and the ones that give students a sense of purpose and competence are more likely to be motivating to them.

Teachers can give their students with dyslexia organisational choices. These are the ones in which students get to choose methods of forming or shaping their learning experiences. Students with dyslexia can choose their own seating; their own study or work partners or groupings; where to work in a classroom and where to stand in line. Teachers can also give their students procedural choices. These are the ones which involve how things are done. Instead of giving all of your classroom a list of 20 spelling words for instance, you can allow your students with dyslexia to choose words from a preapproved list. You can also let your students decide the methods of practising the spelling words instead of assigning the same procedures each week. Giving students with dyslexia real choices in the classroom, whether it is the material they study, the assignments they complete or the peers they work with, will boost their motivation. It allows them to capitalise on their strengths as individual students and enable them to meet their individual learning needs. You can integrate more student choice into your classroom by the choice of books you ask your students to use or read, by the leadership roles or classroom jobs they would like to do inside the classroom and by the assignments they choose to do. Use homework choice boards and ask your students with dyslexia to write about topics that interest them.

Utilise learners' interests

Not all students with dyslexia are motivated by the same desires and needs[3]. Some are simply motivated by receiving support from their other classmates, while others are motivated by overcoming obstacles that appear to hold them back from achieving the accomplishments they desire. Generally, children tend to enter school with high levels of intrinsic motivation. However, this high level of intrinsic motivation tends to decline with time as children progress through their school life. As very young learners, children love to explore their environment as they seek to make sense of the world around them. For those young learners, learning in itself is rewarding. However, learning becomes really fun and engaging when learners are learning about areas and subjects that are of interest and relevance to them. To help your students with dyslexia become avid learners, encourage them to explore topics and subjects that fascinate them. If they like cars, help them find engaging and interesting books, movies and stories about cars. Talk about cars with them and allow them the chance to explain the different makes and models of cars and how they operate. Allow time to discuss your students' interests and what they are learning about now that fascinates them.

The readiness level of your student with dyslexia coupled with his interest generates strong engagement instantly. When students with dyslexia are fully engaged, they spend longer researching matters that interest them and learning more about its content. You cannot really motivate your students with dyslexia depending on their level and type of interests without first knowing what those interests are. It is important to find out from the start of the school year the learning profiles of your students and the areas of interests they care deeply about. These can be done via a number of readily available surveys that you can utilise or by directly asking them. You can also sit with them and ask them directly about the topics and subjects they are most interested in. Be ready to listen to the amazing results of their interests such as playing football, swimming, bike riding, keeping puppies, loving turtles, and of course watching cartoons and playing video games. Teachers can enlist the help of parents to find out what those areas of interests are because they will appear at different times and in different settings. An example of utilisation of students' interests is to ask them to write an essay about their favourite video game. Classify them into groups and get them to discuss what they perceive to be an excellent way to spend their free time and once they finish, they can write a piece of persuasive writing. They get to talk first about something that they like and discuss it, before finally writing an essay about it. This is a recipe for a fun learning experience with many learning objectives achieved.

Provide learners with meaningful experiences

Ensure that you make the content of what is being learned as meaningful as possible. You can do this when your students with dyslexia are offered the opportunity to link their classroom activities to real-life experiences. Innovative activities can really assist a lot in this regard such as storytelling, arts, graphics and mnemonics. Work in a clever way to bring the real world to your classroom. Ask your students to do real-world research; debate on an ongoing topic that is widely known or pressing now. Watch a documentary with them related to the subject matter you are teaching now or listen with them to podcasts and encourage them to publish their work. Teach metacognitive strategies directly and always within the context of meaningful experiences[4].

Adopting a student-centred approach can assist in this regard. When students with dyslexia have the chance and the opportunity to be more involved in designing their own learning experiences, the result is better understanding of the goal of the lesson and more attachment to learning outcomes. Ask your students with dyslexia open-ended questions. Encourage student collaboration and group projects and give them assignments that will allow them to reflect and synthesise what they have learned. Promote self-knowledge because the ultimate goal of learning, as opposed to education, is to help learners function well in society in the future. Encourage the sharing of knowledge and resources among your students with dyslexia and reach out to parents and fellow teachers for ideas and resources that are particularly useful in explaining some of the current materials in your subject matter. Create a bank of classroom materials for your students with dyslexia including lesson plans, videos, PowerPoint presentations, games, puzzles, quizzes and worksheets. Many schools utilise online learning platforms or use external ones that have such resources readily available. Many teachers even collaborate and record those activities so that other teachers can make use of them later.

Set realistic expectations

Motivation is the move towards achieving a goal or fulfilling an expectation. We should always start from the best way to achieve goals, which is to clearly define them. Teachers should always ask their students with dyslexia about their goals and what is it that they would like to achieve. Once your students identify their goal, ask them to write it down. Writing their goal down will always remind them of it. The actual act of writing their goal down will turn their 'I want to achieve this goal' to 'I will achieve this goal'. Once they tell you their goal, you will immediately get a sense of whether this is a short or a long-term goal. Short-term goals are straightforward and can be dealt with easier than long-term goals. Long-term goals, although sound overwhelming sometimes and too distant, can be achieved easily if broken down into smaller more manageable goals. 'How do you eat an elephant? You eat it bite by bite' as the saying goes. How do you achieve a long-term goal? You chip away at the goal by breaking it down into smaller goals which you can achieve little by little. It is therefore important to set realistic expectations for your students.

Encourage your students to raise the following questions when thinking of their goals:

1   When you are thinking about your goal, do you feel that you have the capacity, the necessary energy and above all the motivation to achieve it?
2   What is it that you actually need to achieve your goal?
3   What resources do you have available at your disposal now to achieve your goal?
4   What additional resources do you need more of to assist you in achieving your goal?

Advise your students with dyslexia to always remember to think of and repeat 'I am excited to achieve this goal' rather than simply thinking of it as 'I must do this'. Excitement is motivating. Once their goals are identified, written down and once long-term ones are broken down into shorter ones, then we can assist them by helping transfer their goals into an 'Action Plan'. Action Plans need a schedule to execute and regular monitoring of it[5]. Action Plans also needs to be reassessed and adjusted in order to achieve the goal. Helping learners set realistic, relevant and achievable short and long-term goals is extremely important to motivate learning and retain learners. Student with dyslexia goals should and can be at the forefront of all literacy activities. Students should be active partners in the goal-setting process so that they feel a strong sense of ownership and commitment towards their goals.

Train learners in goal setting

Explain to students that a dream is just a dream but a goal is a dream with a plan and a deadline. If they would like to succeed at school and enjoy their learning journey, they really need to start setting learning and life goals for themselves. Without goals, they would lack focus and direction. That is why goal setting is important because not only it allows them to take control of their own learning direction; but it also provides them with a much-needed benchmark to determine if they are actually succeeding. To accomplish their goals, your students need to know how to set them. One very useful way to think of goal setting is to help students set their own 'SMART' goals: Goals that are Specific; Measurable; Attainable; Realistic and Tangible. Helping students with dyslexia to set short-term goals where they can quickly experience success is a useful strategy. Goal setting is a process that starts with careful consideration of what you want to achieve, and ends with a lot of hard work to actually do it. Knowing those steps will allow your students with dyslexia to formulate goals that they can accomplish. Goal setting is a type of self-awareness method that has been used with children with dyslexia as well as those with negative behaviours[6]. Research identified positive effects of training in goal setting for students with dyslexia and ADHD[7]. Growth-based goals that focus on personal progress can encourage students with dyslexia to consider growth in their own learning[8]. Personal goals can be a way of increasing motivation even in those students who may be particularly prone to poor levels of motivation.

Goal setting training starts with an effective assessment process which is a vital tool for keeping students engaged and retaining them. It also enables teachers to first understand and then support the learning goals and needs of each student. When setting goals for themselves, train your students that it is important that such goals motivate them. To do this, it is very important to ensure that those goals are important to them and that there is indeed value for them in achieving such goals. If they have no or little interest in the outcome, the goals will not work and will not motivate them. To make sure that goals are motivating, train your students to actually write down *why* it is valuable and important to them. Train them to always ask the question: 'If I were to share my goal with others, how can I convince them that it is a worthwhile goal?'.

Publicise goals

If you have ever made a 'New Year's resolution', then you know for sure that keeping such a resolution a secret makes it easier for us to give it up. Making goals visible to others makes our commitment more binding and serious. The same applies to your students with dyslexia who are more likely to reflect on their goals and how to achieve them when they know that others around them are aware of them and will know when it is achieved. One very important way of achieving goals is to hold ourselves accountable. Publicising your goals is doing just that; i.e., I am holding myself accountable by sharing my goals publicly with those around me. It is accountability that really keeps your students with dyslexia striving towards achieving their goal. Accountability gives them a push and increases their focus towards achieving their goals. Accountability is immediately generated and placed once your students make their goals public. You can generate a chart of your students' goals either individually or in small groups. You can always revert back to the same chart to evaluate progress and announce such progress and even reward it.

To increase accountability, one idea that will work very well in school settings is what we name an accountability partner, i.e., someone who is ready and committed to helping your students with dyslexia reach their goals. In return, they can do the same for them. Start an accountability buddy in your class today and try to see if this will encourage and increase motivation among your students with dyslexia because progress goes hand in hand with accountability. Make it easy for your students to take small steps and to keep doing it. Your students are less likely to become overwhelmed from the task at hand and more likely to increase their focus.

Once goals are set and publicised, they are always accompanied by a deadline[9]. Train your students with dyslexia that more important than the deadline is the actual schedule of work; i.e., how are they going to achieve the goal and what steps do they need to take to do so[10]. Often your students are too focused on the actual end goal that sometimes they forget that such a goal is only achieved through a step by step process. That is why it is equally important that once they publicise their goal, they can follow it up by setting a schedule on how they are going to do it. While creating such a schedule, always remember to set small steps in the right direction by breaking down their goal into tiny 'micro-goals' that can be achieved one after the other. Once small steps are achieved, celebrate it with your students because celebrations and good feelings from achieving the small steps enable your students with dyslexia to persevere and push through and carry on with their goal.

Encourage open communication

Communication is a two-way street that is sometimes confused with direction. Direction is one way; i.e., I direct (instruct) you to do a task and little or no discussion is held. Students with dyslexia cannot be directed to be motivated. Motivation factors must be explained and explored through communication between teachers and students. Students elaborate on their goals and motivational factors and teachers assist in explaining what can or cannot be met and why utilising communication. Encourage your students with dyslexia to express their opinion about what is going on with their education. Create an open atmosphere where they feel comfortable expressing their likes, dislikes or concerns. When they share their opinions, make sure to validate their feelings even if you disagree with them. When students with dyslexia feel that their opinion does not matter, or feel that they are stuck, they will be more likely to disengage from learning. Good learners know their opinion matters and feel reassured that they can be open about their educational experience without being judged, put down, discouraged or ignored. Always be open with your communication as students with dyslexia like to be informed and be involved.

Teach constructive communication skills to your students with dyslexia and apply open communication in your relationships with them. This encourages independence rather than dependency. One of the many essential roles teachers assume are that of the inspiration and role model. We all have been introduced to so many teachers during the course of our life. However, we tend to remember one or two in particular with fondness and admiration. Those are the teachers who really cared for us and taught us some very valuable life lessons. Those were almost like mentors for us because they inspired us. They communicated effectively with us and helped us along the way. They inspired us to be even greater than ourselves. They could not have achieved that without first communicating with us in a clear and effective way. They motivated us to love school, to love their subject matter and to love their personality, which in turn inspired us to become more like them. Effective communication will no doubt result in motivating students with dyslexia and changing their mood and desire to work and study.

Focus on learning

It is unfortunately common nowadays for education to generally focus on grades and performance rather than learning. Grades are merely an account in either points or letters of what students earned after completing a particular test or quiz or after handing back their homework. It is far better for us to change the student mindset which is currently focused on reaching a particular percentage and instead empower them to take charge of their learning and measure their own success. Instead of asking your students with dyslexia how they did on their maths test, have them tell you how much they enjoy learning about maths. Focus on what your students with dyslexia are learning, as opposed to how they are performing. While performance is important, focusing on the learning experience will communicate to your students that:

1   Actual learning is more important and fun than test grades;
2   Results are not the most important thing, but learning is;
3   You care more about your students than you do about their performance; and
4   Focusing on the actual learning experience itself will provide them the opportunity to put into their own words their lesson and solidify what they have learned.

Teachers should change their practices from an 'assessment of learning' focus to an 'assessment for learning' focus. A study conducted to identify the effect of letter grades versus comments only or both on students' motivation found that students who received only comments significantly increased their performance[11]. Students who received grades as well as comments and those who received grades only did less well than those who received only comments. Checking in regularly on students' understanding is more helpful than an end-of-unit summary of mastery. Based on this, some teachers opt not to put grades on the top of their students' quizzes and only depend on comments to provide them with timely feedback. Teachers have to remember that they have to make up their mind regarding what is more important: For their students to learn something or simply to take an exam and pass through? By making such a distinction in their minds, teachers can then differentiate between performance goals and learning goals. With performance goals the priority is to get good marks and avoid unfavourable judgements and to also outperform others or avoid being considered incompetent. On the contrary, with learning goals, the priority is to increase competence.

Focus on strengths

'Everyone is a genius but if you judge a fish on its ability to climb a tree, it will live its whole life believing it is stupid' is a famous quotation by Albert Einstein. This quote highlights the importance of us focusing on the strengths of our students and taking their strengths as our springboard from which we can plan, execute and evaluate their learning. We all know and appreciate that focusing on strengths can be difficult when there is so much your student with dyslexia is struggling with academically. However, focusing on their strengths is vital if we are seeking sound emotional and academic improvement. Focusing on our own strengths opens our minds. Once we feel good regarding our own mental capacities and capabilities, we can start using more areas of our brain and we start seeing more options for doing and thinking about things. A happy, positive and relaxed brain can be really creative and focusing on our own strengths increases our brain activity and releases dopamine which in turn makes us feel happy as well as enable us to stay alert for longer and react faster to new information.

On the other hand, focusing on the student's weakness causes them stress which in turn discourages them from further learning. Whatever we hold in our mind and focus on, tends to materialise and the same applies to our own strengths and weaknesses. If we train or teach our students with dyslexia to only focus on their weaknesses, that will make their brains believe that they are merely not good enough and this feeling will strengthen further in their own mind which makes them believe they are incapable of learning or performing or comprehending tasks at hand. That is why focusing on weaknesses in fact stresses the brain because the brain activity is simply trying to resist this feeling of being useless and not good enough. The energy is spent on resisting this feeling rather than being spent on trying to actually understand or comprehend the learning content.

To start focusing on strengths; you have to first find your strength. You can find the points of strengths among your students with dyslexia by simply asking their family and friends about it or by observing them yourself and focusing on what they really enjoy and what makes them bored or disinterested. You can conduct a test to find this information out. There are many such tests available; some for free while others are paid and some are pen and paper while others are electronic.

Remember your achievements

Teach your students with dyslexia to try and memorise their past successes and achievements and let them flow through their mind instead of their failures. Tell them to go and get their past awards, trophies and certificates out and look at them and try and remember their feelings when they received them. Those mementos are a great reminder of past successes. They help motivate us and keep us afloat during times when we are feeling low and unmotivated. Once these are felt again or looked at again and the memories are remembered again, they immediately generate confidence in us as we start to realise that if we have been successful then, we can do it again and become successful now. Those past successes do not even have to be related to the current tasks at hand. If your student with dyslexia is feeling low now and is having a bad day or a bad week, but they were in fact a swimming champion, advise them to get their pictures out and swimming trophy out and look at it again and remember the times when they celebrated them and when people around were cheering for them. This generates a feeling of 'I can do it' and affects their positive attitude. Success generates success and if we have achieved success in the past, remembering such success in the past helps rekindle the feeling of success now and the feeling of self-confidence now.

Although focusing on those achievements for your students with dyslexia may be of help, it is better to in fact focus on what they did in order to achieve those outcomes. Train your students that rather than remembering the day they passed their exam, instead think of such things as the effort they exerted when they were studying. They should also be encouraged to remember the interest they had in the subject, or the way they felt in control of themselves as they worked. Encourage your students to read about heroes they like. Encourage them to watch them and listen to them. Find out what those heroes did that was extraordinary and what made them successful. Remind your students that those were people just like us and that your students can make it and achieve success too. Remembering their previous achievements and following the stories of their heroes motivate your students with dyslexia; so utilise this fact to motivate your students.

Celebrate your achievements

It does not matter how small the achievements of your student with dyslexia is; it is always important to recognise and celebrate it. This applies to every learner but more so for primary stage children who require consistent positive feedback to keep them motivated to learn and challenge themselves to do better. If they finish a difficult project, then they deserve a special treat. If they do well on a literacy or a math test, they can get ice cream or play for 15 minutes. Always recognise their achievements and celebrate them. Celebrating achievements give students a wonderful and amazing feeling of happiness and competence. This feeling is particularly strong when the achievements are noticed by someone else and not just themselves. If that other person does not stop at just noticing but also proceeds to celebrate this with them, the rush of good positive energy is amplified and their feelings of motivation are increased.

Celebrating achievements increases self-confidence and improves school attendance and learning engagement. One important advice to look for when celebrating achievements is to ensure that it is appropriate for the students involved. A celebration of achievement by getting your student with dyslexia a gift that he does not want will have no positive effect on them. Ensure that you think carefully when planning to recognise and celebrate your students' achievements, especially regarding what they like and do not like and what they perceive to be of value to them at this present time. Simply ask your students with dyslexia about what they prefer to have and what a good celebration for them looks like.

Setting up a Hall of Fame is a wonderful way that students with dyslexia love to celebrate their achievements and recognise them. They all like to be mentioned as Student of the Week or Student of the Month or their names to appear on the Dean's List for high achievers. Halls of Fames must be based on a number of criteria and not only one, otherwise you will end up having the same one or two students in the hall of fame all the time which is in itself disheartening for the rest of your class. Awards ceremonies are excellent and ones that are shared by the whole school are even better. Gathering the whole class together to acknowledge the success of your student with dyslexia can be a powerful statement. A round of applause can be uplifting and very encouraging for students. Verbal encouragement and praise are also very easy and inexpensive ways to celebrate students' achievements. Give a pep talk to your struggling students with dyslexia before working on an assignment and verbally celebrate students' who have worked hard to complete a project. Write a personal note to some of your students that you are extremely pleased with. It is timeless and they love it and it motivates them when celebrating their achievements.

Tell a pertinent story

Students love a good story. We all do, and we all enjoy listening to one and watching one. As a teacher, utilise this to your advantage. Be ready with videos and short films of great stories that are inspiring for your students. Be prepared and practise telling a relevant story that is inspirational and motivational in nature. Familiarise yourself with the story and do not rush in telling it. Mastermind your inspirational stories and always keep some handy to assist you in situations where telling a story captures your audience, draws their attention and increases their motivation. Do not rush while telling the story. Hurriedly presented stories reduce their impact and potential benefit. It is not just about what you say in your story, it is also how you say it. If you would like your story to be effective, use your body language and your intonation to convey the emotion you seek to replicate or explain. Have a narrative structure to your story and differentiate between its beginning, middle and end. Tell your story a few times in practice and master the art of your story telling because students with dyslexia love stories and learn a lot from their moral values and inner messages. Stories are easier to remember and easier to learn from. Learning from stories is fun and lasts longer.

Most of the best stories in life generally contain more or less the same simple ingredients: Good characters, difficult problems or challenges, folks trying to solve that problem and finally a powerful conclusion. Start by identifying the message you would like to communicate to your students with dyslexia and search for stories that you can tell which capture your message and bring it to life so that your students understand it. Tell a story that is positive in tone; particularly a story that is true or about real events. Create tension in your story in order to retain your students' attention and also keep your story short and simple. You are lucky because there are so many famous and influential people with documented cases of dyslexia who have talked about their challenges with dyslexia, given interviews about it or even written books about their experiences. Know all of those documented cases of famous people with dyslexia specially the inspiring ones. Use such stories to motivate your students with dyslexia. Focus on the various strategies and feelings those famous people encountered and also on their challenges to reassure your students that they are not alone and that those people overcame their challenges and persevered and achieved their potentials and that your students can do the same too.

Start by doing something small

'The journey of a thousand miles starts from beneath your feet' is taken from verse 64 of the Tao Te Ching by Lao Tzu[12]. In spite of the enormity of the task at hand or how big our students' aspirations and objectives are, they have to start somewhere. That is why it is very important to explain to your students with dyslexia that they have to start somewhere, and that procrastination is one of the biggest obstacles to motivation and achievement. Breaking down a big task into smaller chunks and turning a big objective into small steps allows for the process to start. Although it is reported in the motivation literature to think big, it is also equally important to differentiate between thinking big and performing big or taking big actions at the same time. Due to the progressive nature of some knowledge or certain skills, a scope and sequence is required to perform certain tasks and acquire some skills. You can too, go through these one by one first and that is why it is equally important to start small and build on achievements you gain to continue. There is nothing wrong with thinking big, but when it comes to taking action and making progress, starting small is the key. Teach your students with dyslexia that every master was once a beginner. To make a new habit stick, make sure you start small. Starting small is the key to make actions easier to carry out and lower resistance to them. When your students with dyslexia do small easy things, they tend to just do it and not question themselves or their abilities.

Flow[13] is the state you are in when you work in an enjoyable project or perform a task that makes you happy and you lose your sense of time. Some refer to this as being 'in the zone'. It is a happy enjoyable state and one that is characterised by focusing on the present and the now. Flow comes about on the back of two important factors: Goals and feedback. Students with dyslexia who perform tasks perceived to be at the right degree of challenge for them experience optimal flow. Students who also have clear short-term goals and receive good frequent feedback regarding their progress also tend to achieve optimal flow. Those students enjoy being in control of the task at hand and equally enjoy receiving the good feedback they receive regarding their progress. For your students with dyslexia to achieve this state of flow, you simply need to get them started by doing smaller things such sharpening their pencils or organising their books. When they perform those smaller tasks, they will feel more vigilant and ready for the next big task. They just need to get started to get motivated. If your students with dyslexia do not feel like doing anything sometimes, begin with something small and create a flow of work and motivation.

Do the hardest task first

There are various reasons some students with dyslexia consider certain tasks harder than others. Certain tasks may require prolonged focused time which they find challenging or such tasks may require a combination of skills that are equally challenging for some students with dyslexia to tackle simultaneously. Some tasks require effort in addition to focus. Students with dyslexia are different in the way they approach those tasks. While some students start with the easy ones first then move on to more difficult ones, others address the difficult ones first. People have opposing views about this; however, it is advisable and recommended to encourage your students with dyslexia to start with the difficult tasks first to get it out of the way. If they do the toughest task first, then it will ease a lot of their daily worries and enhance their self-confidence for the rest of the day.

Starting with the hardest task first will always ensure that your student with dyslexia has more time to actually complete it. On the other hand, if they push it back until later, it is more likely that it will be pushed back to the following day or pushed back for longer periods of time or forever. Doing the hardest task first will also guard them against decision fatigue which tends to appear after a long day of work. Students feel relief and joy when they clear their to do tasks, especially when those tasks are the hardest on their to do list. Such a feeling of achievement, relief and joy creates more momentum for them to carry on and keep on working and therefore increases their motivation. It is far more enjoyable for them to spend the rest of the time feeling happy than dreading that difficult task. Furthermore, their achievement makes them happy, so they tend to work faster for the remainder of their task because happiness begets happiness. In addition, students with dyslexia, like the rest of us, have a certain amount of time before they become unproductive. This unproductivity affects their mood and the time taken to perform their tasks. To avoid this, they should be encouraged the get the important things done first.

Train your students with dyslexia not to jump into a task at full speed. Instead, they should start slow and increase the speed as they go along. Starting fast is impulsive and they may lose important details regarding the task at hand. Starting fast emanates from visualising the task as something hard that they have to do it fast. If they imagine the task to be too difficult or the time too short to complete it, their performance and delivery will be negatively affected and they may not even start. On the other hand, getting started, even if it's at a slow pace, is much better than not getting started at all. Sometimes, it is the actions that we do that actually leads to motivation, which in turn leads to more action. So, try and encourage your students to start sometimes before they feel ready. They may then feel more motivated which will enable them and encourage them to take more action. Starting before they feel motivated is understandably difficult.

Incentivise

Incentives pull people towards behaviours that lead to rewards. Similarly, students with dyslexia are pushed away from actions that might lead to negative consequences. Two students may act in totally different ways given the same situation and that is based entirely on the types of incentives that are available to them at that time[14]. Some students study for an exam to achieve a good grade while others are after recognition. Such actions are based on the basic premise that there will be something obtained in return for efforts exerted. For example, children love to eat and whether they are elementary or secondary school students, inviting them for a pizza is a great incentive. The Pizza Hut company in the US has been providing pizza to incentivise students to read for almost 40 years now. They offer free pizzas for students who reach their reading goals. Although some felt that this is controversial and might be sending the wrong signal that reading is in itself unpleasant and needs to be encouraged by an incentive, the programme is still going strong and many teachers find that it helps to get students to read. Once students start reading, their fluency increases and their vocabulary knowledge increases which in turn helps them become better readers[15].

The incentive can be simply a pizza treat or a ribbon to be worn around the school for everyone to see. The ribbon or coat can say they are the Star or the Hero of the Week or the Day. Students with dyslexia love those incentives. Many students like to become members on the student council or members of the end of the year graduation ceremony or members of the Christmas play. Whatever the occasion, use this fact to incentivise them. They like to be recognised and they like to be special and they like to be chosen and remembered. This is very rewarding for them as it makes others look at them with respect and admiration and a way for them to feel special. Incentives work, so use them. In their 'Power and Pitfalls of Education Incentives' published in 2011, Allan & Fryer[16] investigated the effects of financial incentives on academic performance in schools in the US. Their study offered students money for reading books, taking exams or improving grades in core subjects. Students who were paid money for each book they read showed improvement in their literacy skills at the end of the school year. However, students who were paid money to take exams or improve class grades showed little improvement. The authors conclude that rewarding *behaviour,* such as reading books, can be a sufficient incentive for students but paying for *results*, such as better grades, appears to do little to motivate them.

Give accurate feedback

Feedback is the information provided by teachers regarding aspects of their students' performance or understanding and as such feedback is a 'consequence' of student performance[17]. Feedback plays a major role in motivating students when feedback terms used do not lead students to consider errors as indicative of ineffective strategies or insufficient effort from their part[18]. Teachers can boost their students' motivation by providing accurate feedback that is specific to the task at hand[19]. Feedback does not happen in a vacuum though; i.e., to increase the effectiveness of their feedback, teachers should note that there must be a learning context in which feedback is given. Therefore, saying 'well done' or a 'good job' generally and casually should be avoided and is not regarded as accurate feedback. Instead, say 'good job for …' and provide reasons for your feedback. Say 'well done because …' and provide accurate scenarios or performance situations that you observed and liked and which prompted you to say well done in the first place. Positive feedback or praise that is insincere or not justified nor deserved should be avoided. Instead, teachers are encouraged to point out areas that need improvement to assist their students with dyslexia.

Because teachers' feedback to students with dyslexia is in itself a consequence of their students' performance, there are two extreme forms of feedback: One that is very distinctive from instruction provided by the teacher, and at the other extreme end feedback becomes an integral part of the actual instruction. Regardless of which end the feedback lies, it is important that it is accurate and specific to the task at hand. When delivered accurately, feedback can improve students' performance and aid their learning. Accurate feedback can also help students understand their strengths and weaknesses and enable them to implement strategies to improve their performance. Accurate feedback is most powerful when it addresses faulty interpretations or faulty understanding and not a lack of understanding. When giving accurate feedback, teachers are advised to not only focus on areas of improvement, but also mention areas where the learner is excelling. If the focus of the feedback, regardless of how accurate it is, is always on the areas of improvement only, students will feel demotivated and devalued. Therefore, accurate feedback regarding areas of improvement should always be accompanied by accurate feedback regarding areas that students with dyslexia are strong in or the ones that they have shown progress and achievement in too.

Give positive feedback

Giving frequent positive feedback that supports students' beliefs that they can do well is very important in the learning process[20]. On the other hand, negative teacher feedback given to students on a regular basis was found to predict students' lack of motivation and, subsequently, poor academic performance[21]. Both negative and positive comments influence motivation, though students with dyslexia are more affected by positive feedback and success. Students with dyslexia who are led to believe that their failures reflect a lack of ability on their part will, as a result, become less motivated and less persistent to face new challenges. Teachers can avoid such negative and undesired results when giving their feedback if they focus on the feedback terms that they use. Those feedback terms should ensure that students are well aware that their errors indicate ineffective strategies or insufficient efforts rather than inadequate ability.

Praise builds students' self-confidence and competence. Students with dyslexia are motivated when their sincere efforts are recognised even if their learning outcomes are less than optimal. When your students with dyslexia perform below your expectation, inform them clearly that they should try and improve this over a period of time that you can agree with them. Show them examples of good work done by their classmates to clarify effort level and what is expected of them. This is a realistic technique to enable the less motivated students to appreciate the required level of input and effort from their teachers.

Feedback regarding students' effort was found to increase their motivation, whereas feedback regarding the teachers' perceived intelligence level of the student decreased motivation. Some teachers have a built-in model to give their feedback. They first start with the positive element of their feedback before they introduce the constructive or negative feedback component. They then close with the specific feedback elements that builds up their students' trust and comfort. Other teachers use a different model of feedback so they begin by identifying the exact learning situation the feedback refers to then they proceed to define the specific behaviours that they would like to address with their students with dyslexia before finally describing how their students' behaviours impacted them or others around them. Regardless of the type or process you utilise to give the feedback to your students with dyslexia, use more positive ones and use them more frequently as it is very helpful for their motivational level.

Reinforce learning through repetition

Getting your students to do more work and stay longer at a task and try harder is a daily occurrence in school life. It is important for effective teachers to get their students with dyslexia to 'do more' than they think they can do or believe they are capable of doing. To this end, an important lesson all teachers learn early on during their teaching career is to deliver their message in different ways. They explain a point in their lesson in more than one way and they give examples and sometimes ask students to repeat or explain it in their own words. As well as being a good teaching practice, repetition is an important aspect of learning as it literally paves the way for smoother information processing. Neurons on our brain link and join together to form a neuronal pathway; i.e., ultimately a super information highway that information coming from our senses utilise to reach the various information processing centres in the brain. Neurons produce a glue/adhesive like substance which enables them to attach/stick to nearby neurons. It is by repetition that this glue is produced. Repetition is therefore at the heart of all learning. So, even if you are short for time, look for opportunities to revisit and review the learning content.

There is a wide variety of ways in which an idea can be repeated: A teacher can repeat it orally in class, in writing before or after class, or informally outside of class. A student can repeat it in class, in learning teams or out of class. The same information can be contained in the course materials/books and additional readings or by a visiting speaker. Design your teaching and explanations like a story that has a few major themes to be repeated frequently, and a number of subsidiary ideas to be built. Great stories have a beginning to encourage curiosity, a middle that provides the essence and an ending that summaries both. Hasher et al. (1977)[22] coined the term Illusion of Truth or (IOT for short) upon their discovery that statements repeated even once are rated as truer or more valid than statements heard for the first time. Therefore, even a single repetition can apparently make information appear more valid. A feeling of familiarity is produced by repetitions and any factor that generates a typically nonconscious sense of familiarity automatically and unintentionally increases validity[23]. The learning process is one of slow engagement with ideas; gradually the engagement builds to a critical mass when the student actually acquires the idea. Repetition matters because it can hasten and deepen the engagement process. If one cares about quality of learning, one should consciously design repetitive engagement into courses and daily teaching.

Do not expect to feel motivated all the time

An important way to deal with a lack of motivation among your students with dyslexia is to stop expecting them to feel motivated all the time. No one feels motivated all the time. Do not rely on your students' feeling motivated to get the work done because sometimes the motivation will not be there. If sometimes you try everything and you still seem unable to motivate them, shift your focus and start working with them on developing a study routine and study habits. Study routines and study habits are systems that you can build to assist your students with dyslexia when they lose their motivation. Sometimes, a lack of motivation can indicate that they either need a break or they need a change. Sometimes your students with dyslexia wear themselves out trying to be the best at everything. For your students with dyslexia to experience such a feeling of sloth sometimes is OK and normal. After all, we are all human and are not meant in fact to work ourselves to death. So, if you see that your student is not motivated sometimes and the usual ideas and advice are not working, you might need to stop for a short while and take time with them to reflect why. They might be wanting to do too much too soon, or they may simply need a break for their body to relax.

Remember that motivation is an emotion just like other emotions such as sadness, fear, anger, happiness and everything else you feel. Just like those emotions, motivation does not last forever. Even the most motivated students feel unmotivated sometimes and do not experience endless motivation[24]. Students have good days and bad days sometimes and can sometimes experience negative emotional patterns that may affect their overall motivation. Train your students to get over the fact that although they might not feel like it, they still have to do it sometimes. This is where the work routine and study habits pay off. Once your students with dyslexia understand that motivation is just an emotion like other emotions, they proceed to then ask themselves the important follow up questions: Can they still go on with their work and study although they do not feel like it?; i.e., can they work regardless of their emotion? The answer to this question is yes, as they can and nothing is really holding them back when they work even though they do not feel like it sometimes. This may be the right attitude to combat lack of motivation sometimes. It is OK not to feel 100% motivated as no one does feel motivated 100% all the time. However, motivation is just an emotion and they need to get on with their work and their assignments and although it is difficult and easier said than done, we all have to do something we do not really enjoy at the moment because it has to be done and because it is the right thing to do.

Notes

1 Stipek, 1996.
2 Guthrie et al., 2000.
3 Martin, 2009.
4 Wray, 1994.
5 Elliot & Dweck, 1988.
6 Linnenbrink-Garcia et al., 2008.
7 Maehr & Zusho, 2009.
8 Ratey & Sleeper-Triplett, 2011.
9 Ames, 1992.
10 Locke & Latham, 2002.
11 Butler, 1988.
12 www.wussu.com/laotzu/laotzu64.html.
13 For further information, refer to Csikszentmihalyi's (2009) book *Flow*.
14 Covington, 2002.
15 Willingham, 2008.
16 www.scholarchip.com/incentive-for-students.
17 Hattie & Timperley, 2007.
18 Lepper & Chabay, 1985.
19 Linnenbrink & Pintrich, 2003.

20 Davis, 1999.
21 Wentzel, 1997.
22 Hasher, Goldstein & Toppino, 1977.
23 Begg et al., 1992.
24 Breen & Lindsay, 2002.

8 Motivate students with dyslexia by understanding learning

Learning environment: Seating

The physical setup of chairs and tables in a classroom can significantly influence learning. A classroom should be an adaptable and a flexible setting where teachers can make an arrangement for the tables, chairs and materials to stimulate active involvement during lessons. Teachers should decide which location is the best to stimulate an individual student's academic and social development, while encouraging interaction and reducing distractions[1]. Teachers are responsible for making decisions regarding the grouping of students within their classrooms[2]. They determine which students sit close to each other, who they are exposed to and with whom they interact during the school day. Spaces designed in a student-centred manner that focus on learner construction of knowledge can indeed support student learning[3]. Students get to spend a lot of time in a classroom. Their desks are arranged in a particular way and their individual seats tend to be determined by their teacher[4]. This is indeed part of the bigger classroom management tasks as teachers face the question of how and where to seat their students[5]. It is an important decision because classroom seating arrangements are found to influence classroom climate as well as relationships between students[6]. Research suggests that students with dyslexia tend to prefer more flexible seating arrangements[7].

Teachers are encouraged to consider ways to modify seating arrangements and match them with the demands of classroom activities to help maximise student learning. Match classroom seating arrangement to the goals of your instruction. Classes involving group work can utilise group tables as opposed to whole class discussion which would benefit from a horseshoe shape seating arrangement. Strategically change arrangements during class to suit shifting learning goals but ensure not to do it in such a way that it takes too long or it creates chaos, noise or disturbs the flow of the class. Ensure the child with behaviour and distraction problems is positioned as close to you as possible and away from large windows or open doors. Designate time for setting up the classroom and ask students to help. A seating arrangement in rows compared to groups can instigate positive academic behaviours such as hand-raising and complying with requests. Rows can support students' on-task behaviour during independent work.

Learning environment: Scenery

A classroom is a great place for learning, but sitting at the same desk every day can be boring and dull for some students. Renew interest in your subject matter by giving your students with dyslexia the chance to get out of their classroom sometimes. Field trips are excellent opportunities for you to do so. You can invite guest speakers to address them or you can visit the library to do some research with your students. If your school has a garden or a cafeteria or a computer room, hold your occasional class there[8]. If moving your students is not possible for you, try including music, films or podcasts in your lessons to change your scenery. You can always change the configurations of the desks and chairs inside the classroom or change the groups of the students who work with each other. Let your students with dyslexia search for their seats when they come in the classroom. You can also start a competition among your students for the design of a new bulletin board. This board should display learning going on in the classroom and celebrate the various achievements of your students. Students with dyslexia love to have their work displayed in front of other students as it makes them feel proud.

Ask your students with dyslexia where they would like to sit and transfer them from time to time? Occasionally, you can also change the decorations inside your classroom. Involve your students with dyslexia in making wall charts and posters and change them regularly so that there is always something new to notice. Make the classroom space about your students and let there be evidence of their learning. Do some work in the playground or inside the PE hall/gymnasium. Working in a different environment will help keep your students on their toes. The more you encourage movement in learning, the more the information is absorbed. Learning can be done anywhere, and experiences make lasting learning.

When taking your students out, whether outside the classroom to another space inside the school grounds or outside of the school grounds, ensure that the places they are going to are connected to what is going on in the classroom; i.e., create relevance with learning. That way, they will be more likely to remember the information. Teachers should adopt more experiential approaches to learning and education in general and changing the scenery allows them to do so with their students with dyslexia. During such instances, students with dyslexia get the chance to actively use the outdoor atmosphere and ambience to apply the theoretical knowledge they learned and undertake problem solving chances in real world situations.

Learning environment: Distractions

Most students with dyslexia struggle with distractions to some degree inside the classroom. Teachers observe distractions in different forms such as phones, iPods, iPads, computers, social media websites, video games, friends, noise or even internal thoughts. Many students with dyslexia struggle to stay focused and end up not getting the most benefit out of their classes due to distractions. Many students with dyslexia study with one eye on their textbook and the other eye on their social media feed. Some of them try to text each other while in class or start browsing the internet or using social media networks. Such an addiction some students have to social media networks can have a negative impact on their learning and can increase their distractions from the task at hand or from learning in general. Some students, while listening to their lessons partially, are online with their laptops or smart phones and they spend a lot of their time checking their own home page or status. Their ability to pay attention to one person or one thing is negatively affected because of their heavily involvement in social media.

There are a few steps that can be taken to alleviate this depending on the rules and regulations adopted in your academic institution. You can of course always turn off internet access or ask your students to put their phones on flight mode. Alternatively, they can put their phone in another room or not be allowed to take it out of their bag while at school. They can also mute their group chats or use earplugs. Sometimes, it is advisable that they delete all the games on their phone, tablet or computer. They can also ask their friend, roommate or classmate to keep them accountable to their goals and fight against distractions. They can give their phone or laptop to a friend to hold onto when they are studying. Or they can try studying with a friend or a group to hold each other accountable to staying on task. They can also limit or bar themselves from unnecessary technology use during study and class times.

As a teacher, you can remove distracting items such as sporting equipment, games and art materials during classroom instruction. You can post a 'Do Not Disturb' sign on your classroom door during important activities such as tests or exercises that require a great deal of concentration. Always take time to ensure that other teachers and school staff honour your classroom rules and boundaries. You can advise your students with dyslexia to make an appointment with an academic counsellor to create a plan to decrease distractions in their life or to work on other academic issues. Although technology is useful inside the classroom, misuse of technology also negatively affects learning. Therefore, there should be a balance between banning and freeing the use of technology.

Learning environment: Work display

Wall displays are an important part of any classroom, as they make the room appear more inviting and create a better learning environment. Displaying your students' work in the classroom lets them know you value their work and you value them. Documenting the process of your students' work benefits them and engages their parents. Hanging up their work in the classroom is an excellent way to celebrate their efforts! Students with dyslexia feel a great sense of self-worth when something they have written or created is hanging up for others to see. In addition, a classroom filled with the work of children is a delight to be in and sends a message to students that their work and their learning are important. A good display not only engages and informs, it also brightens up the atmosphere of the classroom. A classroom display should not only create an engaging learning and working environment for the students, but should also reflect their teacher's personality and style of teaching.

In addition to having a meaningful connection to the curriculum, displays should also be an effective tool for teaching and learning. Information on display should connect with and expand the knowledge of your students with dyslexia regarding topics being studied. Including 3D elements or games will bring your display to life and involve your students more. Displayed work of your students should be informative and easy for them to understand. Wall displays that are full of texts can be tedious to read. Instead, teachers are encouraged to use keywords and diagrams to get the message across effectively and in an eye-catching manner. Use learning aids and resources on or around your display to help your students with dyslexia learn independently. Students can choose pieces of their own work that they give to teachers to assemble into a display or they can create the actual display themselves.

Setting up a display allows students with dyslexia to develop their creativity and practise related skills such as measuring, cutting, using tools and writing. Furthermore, maintaining displays gives an opportunity for students with dyslexia to develop organisational and decision-making skills. Once children have learned how to choose work for displays and to display work effectively, they may be ready to take over the management of some of the display areas. Although it is important to choose colours and themes that will attract students' attention, it is also important not to overload your display with too many colours and too much information as it may overstimulate students. The location of your classroom display is as important as the information placed on it. Walls are not the only location in a school classroom that are suitable for a classroom display. Teachers can also use: Classroom doors, windows, storage cupboard doors, front panel of your desk, mobile display on wheels or a table-top display and display boards.

Learning content: Relevance

For learning to take place, the learning content must be relevant. We tend to pay special attention to what interests us and what we perceive to be of particular value to us. Relevance is the perception that something is interesting and worth knowing. Relating your subject matter to the real world and making your instruction and teaching methods accessible will increase the overall motivation of your students. Consider having lesson plans and discussions about topics that are prevalent in your students' lives[9]. Challenge your students with dyslexia to write about why what they are learning is relevant. Try project-based learning or presenting learning as a project to your students with dyslexia. In such situations, students are given a question or a task that they need to complete. Typically, completing such a project ensures that there are opportunities for research, group work, community involvement, further reading or even the creation of a product. To teach different text genres for instance or expressive writing, you can classify your classroom into groups and give each a project to have a final piece of writing such as a menu for a restaurant or a petition to the school principal to have a free dress day at school. The more the content is relevant to your students, the easier it is to remember it and enjoy it.

When preparing your lessons, think of a real-world question or a real-world scenario that your students with dyslexia would need to answer and can only do so by learning the content of your lesson. Instead of teaching them the imperative form in the grammar section of your literacy class, ask them to write first a recipe for someone who likes to make pancakes. Teach the imperative form of the verb through this fun recipe so that they understand and use it in a relevant way. You can always use simulations that mimic real-life events. Learning about calculations and basic mathematical operations takes on a new meaning when students are involved in a Monopoly game where they 'buy and sell' houses and districts and calculate how much money they need or each one costs. Field trips are a great way of making learning relevant because rather than having students with dyslexia simply read about something in a textbook, you send them directly to the source material. Aquarium, football clubs, hospitals, museums, fire stations and art galleries are a few examples of how such field trips can make complicated learning fun and enjoyable. It is also good to note that sometimes it is necessary for learners to attach a new piece of information to an old one. Effective teaching helps students recognise patterns and put new information in context with the old ones.

Learning content: Fun

The current digital age has led to an engagement crisis issue for teachers from the side of students who are always on the lookout for fun and motivating content. Therefore, it is critical to be able to keep your students' attention as long as possible on the important things for them. Learning becomes sometimes boring if a traditional education approach places everything in certain frames that cannot be exceeded. Students with dyslexia are constantly told that learning is very serious and fun is the complete opposite of it. When a certain activity becomes boring, students with dyslexia try to entertain themselves with their mobile phones or by playing games. Fun activities should be embraced because that is where the full potential lies. Teachers should teach their students with dyslexia having fun while doing something serious is not bad. One of the critical elements in making learning interesting and fun is a variety of activities and information. If lessons remain the same every day, eventually it will get boring even for top students.

Turning your lesson into a game will always make learning fun. Turn review activities and rote memorisation drills into games. Encourage your students with dyslexia to take breaks during the lesson itself. Expecting the students to keep their attention all throughout the day is a big mistake. Take just a minute or two for students with dyslexia to have a quick bathroom break, refreshments or to avoid distraction during the lesson. Use achievements, leader boards, badges and levels to significantly increase interest in your subject.

Gamification in learning has the biggest chance to make learning fun. Making learning fun is not a hard idea to execute. The important point here for teachers is to pay attention to their students with dyslexia and react to them. Once there is a mutual interest between the teachers and their students, it will be a lot easier to reach the needed goals and the easiest way to do it is through gamification. Gamification is one of the most innovative technological ideas in modern education. Game elements are used to increase their users' involvement and make the whole process more fun. Your students with dyslexia need a personal connection to the learned material. Either engage them emotionally or connect the new information with previously acquired knowledge.

Learning content: Interesting

We all have experiences of studying a subject that we thought was boring. It is difficult to study a boring subject and specially one that you experience failure in. However, some think that there are no boring subjects, but rather disinterested minds. If your students with dyslexia think that your subject is boring, they will not engage with you and it will be hard to motivate them. You can start changing this by first adding some humour into your subject and into your teachings. Humour helps us remember facts because our emotions were that of happiness and fun. You can always make your subject matter spectacular by ensuring that you include infographics, pictures, graphs and audio files that transform the information into various formats that different students can capture and relate to. Make and create a story of all such infographics, photos, graphs and audio files because students with dyslexia always remember a story that is well structured. Teach your students with dyslexia to use highlighters and colour code the textbooks and the important materials inside the texts. Colours are helpful memory joggers when it comes to printed information and help students with dyslexia focus. You can use colours to categorise ideas. You can also colour arrows and graphs and draw a shape to represent the boring information into some meaningful picture. Coloured flashcards are also very useful to aid memory in the case of a boring subject.

Try and use a white background sometimes so that the contrast between colours can stand out. Students' recall recognition of images increases by 5% when the images are in colour[10]. You can also utilise the Pomodoro Technique which was invented in the early 1990s by Francesco Cirillo[11]. The methodology is simple: When faced with a large task, break it down into short, timed intervals that are spaced out by short breaks. This trains the brains of your students with dyslexia to focus for short periods and helps them stay on top of their deadlines. With time it can also help improve their attention span and concentration. This technique has been around for decades. It's really nice and simple. It's a simple way to ensure that your students with dyslexia give themselves brain breaks and then force themselves to focus for a specific period of time. All they need to do is set a timer on their phone for a set amount of time and carry out a piece of focused work.

Allow learners to work together

Assigning group work is a good teaching strategy as indeed by working together in small groups, students with dyslexia get the chance to: Develop their critical thinking skills, exchange their knowledge, share their experiences and improve their attitudes towards learning. While not all students will be excited to work in groups, many will find it fun to try to solve problems, do experiments and work on projects with other students[12]. It is this social interaction that is generated from working together in groups that gets your students with dyslexia excited about learning and about the things they do in the classroom. For this to work, however, teachers need to ensure that groups are balanced and fair so that some students are not doing more work than others. Common student complaints about group work include unequal workloads or group members who work independently rather collaboratively. In most cases, the root cause for students' inability to work in groups may be the fact that many do not know how to work in groups in an effective manner because teachers tend to provide plenty of information about the assignment itself but little on how to get the work done in groups. Without such structure, differences in work style and work ethics may result in the failure of some students with dyslexia to work in small groups and educators who have implemented group work to realise that[13].

To make group work more successful for your students with dyslexia, acknowledge yourself first that group dynamics are important and provide your students with tools to improve how they work together. Call your students with dyslexia who work together teams, not groups. Although a group consists of students who coordinate their individual efforts, a team, however, has a common purpose and a shared responsibility for success. Once they are in teams, give the teams names. Ask your students with dyslexia to come up with a team name for themselves because it is a simple team-building activity in itself. By creating a name for themselves, your students with dyslexia will start developing an identity. Train your students on team building and interpersonal skills. Because group work situations tend to give rise to brainstorming and idea sharing, as a teacher, you will learn a lot about how your students with dyslexia learn best by taking a slightly back seat and observing the learning process as it unfolds in front of you. You can introduce some simple ground rules and learning cycles in order to see improvements in team outcomes. Although introducing an element of competition or reward for the best team can be very motivating for some students, be careful that your groups are evenly matched and all have a fair chance of winning.

Create healthy competition

Competition happens when students compete against each other in an activity, a game or quiz. This can happen individually or if they are grouped in teams. A friendly spirit of competition in your classroom is always welcome and most teachers have tried introducing competition into their classroom. You can introduce a competitive game, a leader board or a contest which often increases students' excitement, energy and enthusiasm. Students with dyslexia see and experience competition in their PE classes regularly and they also experience competition when they audition for a school play or the Christmas production. Creating a sense of competition through games is fun and engaging and it is motivating to your students with dyslexia. Grouping your students into teams, or houses, and having them play against each other and completing a challenge and earning points is always exciting for your students. Which team can generate the most relevant vocabulary to our lesson today? Which group can write the best essay? Or which team can provide the best sentences which contain the correct grammatical structures you are currently explaining?

Regardless of the learning content your students with dyslexia are studying at the moment, there is some way to add some competition to the mix[14]. Such examples are healthy competition that should be encouraged. Winning in such situations is a welcome assurance of ability and understanding but even losing is rewarding and important for some students. In the case of failure, your students with dyslexia can identify the problems and fix the shortcomings. They can also revisit their goals and move forward while benefitting from their experiences. Although students with dyslexia need to feel successful to become and stay motivated, they can also learn from their losses and failures if they are taught that taking part is more important than winning in the competition.

Competition makes learning seem more like a game, which in turn transforms school to being fun and students with dyslexia feel excited to be there. It can also encourage students with dyslexia to be more actively involved in the classroom[15]. Competition in teams may also lead to better cooperation and a sense of community inside the classroom. For students who thrive under pressure, healthy competition works.

Focus on the process

If the aim of your students with dyslexia is to succeed by passing their exam and making it to the next year, this will take them a whole academic year to achieve. For young learners, a whole academic year seems far away to motivate them. Instead, teach your students with dyslexia that success is a journey rather than a destination. When they are focused on the process of their learning, they feel really excited about being in the present and enjoying it more fully. When students with dyslexia are working, it is difficult sometimes for them to see the fruit of their labour, especially at the beginning of the school year and that is why you should teach them to focus on the process, not the result. For your students with dyslexia, focusing on results puts them in partial control of whether they in fact reach it or not. There may be things working against them such as the time available to them or their support group or the competition they face. However, when they do not have the challenge of getting results hovering over them, they start to focus on their own internal locus of control which leads to higher self-esteem and empowerment. All this happens when they stop focusing on the results and start focusing on the process of learning itself.

Ask your students with dyslexia: Did they complete most of their planned tasks for today? If yes, advise them to congratulate themselves. Did they stick to their study schedule today? If not, advise them to maintain their focus. When your students with dyslexia start focusing their attention and energy less on the results but rather on the processes or the techniques involved, they will discover that they learn faster and become more successful. Because mistakes are part of existence, mistakes help your students with dyslexia learn and grow in life. When they are focused on a specific desired result, they become less willing to experiment or take risks that may just push them to a better outcome than the one they were actually aiming for. Some parents place an unnecessary burden on their children to deliver results. Those students act as if they are really pushed to prove a point and might end up cutting corners to achieve such results. However, when those students start focusing on the process, they immediately eliminate the noise of such external factors. Because there is less pressure, learning becomes less about winning or losing and more about gaining mastery in what they are learning.

Learning as a process is rewarding in itself and there is happiness in enjoying the fruit of learning. That is what focusing on the process gives your students with dyslexia. There is no point in placing their entire success on only a specific outcome. Rather, train your students with dyslexia to let their happiness be dependent on how much they have worked and enjoyed the process to reach it rather than the result itself.

Create a study routine

By nature, we are all creatures of habit, so when your students with dyslexia are experiencing some challenges to get motivated to study, put this principle to work for you. It is generally easier to stay motivated if their studying becomes part of their everyday life and routine because habits are powerful and once your students with dyslexia develop a study routine, they will find it difficult to go into relaxation mode without studying. Once habits are established, they do not require willpower to keep in motion; that is why habits are more effective than self-discipline. So, your task as a teacher is to help them create a study routine. There are so many tips to create a study routine. We shall focus on some that are useful and easier to implement for your students with dyslexia. Train your students to set up a study schedule.

Before you train your students with dyslexia to create their own study routine, help them first find out what there dominant learning style is. It is important for your students to know that there are many different styles of learning and each one of them will retain information better in different ways. They need to figure out which style of learning works best for them as this will help them determine how to study, where to study and when to study. Once their learning style is known, advise your students with dyslexia to start creating and writing down their realistic study goals. Some questions to ask themselves may help create realistic goals and come up with a plan for a good study habits are: When do they usually study? How long do they normally study for? What subjects do they need to focus on? Which subjects are they having the most difficulty with? What are the grades they need to pass? Once those questions are answered, it will become clearer for them which areas they need to focus on.

Train your students with dyslexia that sooner is better than later always when it comes to study habits. Ask them to get things done as far in advance as they possibly can. Doing things early ensures that they will always have time ahead of them which gives them the option to make their own choices. The more they get done now, the more time they have to prepare for exams later. Doing things in smaller chunks is a brilliant study habit that saves your students with dyslexia time. When they have big goals, the earlier they start the better. Train them to pick the next thing on their list and just start because taking small steps is the best cure for procrastination. Just advise them to get something done because most of them wait until right before the due date to get started. Getting lots of things done gives them a continuous sense of progress. If putting all of their study time into a few days before the exams is not working for them, then perhaps it is time for them to try something less stressful. They can make time for studying every day, whether they have exams coming up or not. Consistency is a good study habit that they will be able to maintain throughout the school year.

Collect clear data

Clear data regarding students and their progress, i.e., their learning styles, aspirations and interests, are useful for teachers who use it to drive their decisions and plans to respond to problems more effectively. It also aids teachers to try new teaching methods and advance their skills faster. By collecting data and saving it digitally, teachers can instantly refer to it throughout the year and compare performance between years[16]. Teachers are advised to keep data they collect basic by using simple techniques that connect with each other. They can start small and scale their efforts with progress. Once teachers find methods that work well for them, they should apply them systematically to all of their classes. Teachers can always analyse their own efforts and reflect on whether the steps they have taken have led to an increase in their students' engagement, achievement or overall satisfaction. Teachers can also encourage their students to reflect upon their own progress by using a graph or a chart. Regardless of the data you collect, be open about communicating with others about your class-wide results. You can do this by relaying information about outcomes and explaining how instruction will be modified based on new data.

Although too much data can be overwhelming and some schools may have a tendency to gather more data than they actually need, gathering no data at all is also not a good practice[17]. How do you otherwise know which method of your teaching is the most successful or which visual aid you are using yields the best results? Which learning objective is harder to cover and which learning style is easier to cater for? How are your students progressing and what percentage of progress is being achieved? Collecting clear data and keeping them and reflecting on them and presenting them in a meaningful way is a great asset to aid teachers. However, it is equally important to note that collecting reliable and accurate data requires discipline from teachers. While some teachers are not comfortable with tracking progress over time, others view interpreting data as an additional burden and that is why it is recommended to collect and analyse data in an actionable way to save time and effort.

Collecting data regarding your students with dyslexia and their progress is an important factor in increasing their achievement despite controversy over privacy and security concerns[18]. Collaborate with others to make your teaching method data driven. There are many technology solutions available now for teachers to make such a process easier and enjoyable. Collecting clear data and modifying instructions accordingly makes learning fun, enjoyable and rewarding which in turn increases motivation.

Assign classroom jobs

If you would like to increase your students' active role inside the classroom and engage them more, an excellent idea is to assign them a classroom job to do. Classroom jobs give your students with dyslexia important responsibilities and increase their sense of ownership and belonging. Rotate the variety of jobs among your students to ensure that everyone is sharing responsibilities and to achieve fairness. Post a list of classroom jobs with student names publicly to clarify which student is responsible for which job. Such a list can be changeable. To teach students with dyslexia to be accountable for themselves, for their belongings and their learning environment, teachers have to trust them with responsibility. Students with dyslexia feel capable when they have a sense of control over their learning environment and when they are making a contribution to the smooth running of their classroom. Classroom jobs facilitate the role of teachers to nurture self-worth and self-esteem and it gives students the opportunity to feel proud of their accomplishments.

There are so many classroom jobs that you can allocate to your students with dyslexia. A supply master keeps learning and classroom supplies organised and alerts the teacher when these need replenishing. A spill detector calmly alerts the teacher in the cases of spills such as juices, paints, experiment solutions and water. The famous board eraser cleans all boards at the end of or throughout the day. The recycling chief ensures that bins are emptied periodically and that recycling is taking place. The classroom blogger writes down important events taking place inside the classroom and documents learning. There are so many other classroom jobs such as the paper handler, special meetings ambassador and the secret admirer. Tell your students with dyslexia you have noticed that there are lots of jobs that need to be done in the classroom to keep it organised, safe and effective for learning purposes. Ask them to reflect on other reasons why it is helpful to keep a tidy and organised classroom. Conclude from your discussions with them that it is really helpful for us as a community inside the classroom to look after our own classroom so that we can enjoy learning together and to be able to find things faster. Think of enough jobs to assign one duty per student. Although some students with dyslexia may not simply know how to put new staples in the stapler at the beginning of the school year, or to feed the lamination machine with laminating sheets, they are happy to help and will soon become your valuable experts in class.

Go the extra mile and design an application form for students with dyslexia to apply for a classroom job. Before announcing jobs in the classroom, organise a formal class meeting to describe each job in detail and focus on the values of responsibility, accountability and trust. Once jobs are assigned and soon after they start, organise performance reviews. Observe your students with dyslexia closely and encourage them when they are performing their jobs well.

Give clear tasks

Teachers are advised to ensure that tasks given to their students with dyslexia are clear and that students know exactly what is required of them to complete the task. Students do not feel in control when they are given a task that they are not sure what is required of them or how to go about completing it. Giving clear instructions to students with dyslexia regarding the tasks required can positively affect their success inside the classroom as when the tasks are clearly identified, they can engage with teaching and learning materials more effectively and have a more productive learning experience[19]. When setting a task, teachers are advised to be clear and allow students with dyslexia time to prepare first and ask any questions. There is nothing more frustrating for students with dyslexia than not being able to perform well because they did not understand the task. Tasks that might be difficult to some students may be easier to others depending on the level of readiness and ability of the students. It is therefore highly recommended that teachers prepare various tasks with various difficulty levels to facilitate the differentiation of their own teaching accordingly.

There are several advice ideas teachers can adopt to ensure that their students with dyslexia understand fully the required task. First, teachers are always encouraged to use clear and precise language. Use short, complete sentences and concrete terms to enable your students with dyslexia to understand what you expect of them. Teachers are also advised to clearly articulate their expectations from the task. Explain to your students with dyslexia what they need to do, how to do it and when it has to be done by. Once teachers clearly communicate what is required, they are advised to repeat their directions. Write the task and also say the task and then ask one of your students with dyslexia to explain what is required and use those repetitions to clarify the task. Teachers are also advised to explain the rationale and the purpose of the task and ensure that their students with dyslexia are listening and paying attention when they are doing so. Sometimes, teachers may resort to a different tone of voice in order to stress certain situations like explaining the homework or the task at hand. Teachers are also always advised to use examples when making the tasks clearer to their students with dyslexia.

Explain task rationale

Whether your students are working by themselves 'seatwork' or working with other members of the classroom 'group work', they are engaged in some assignment that you have asked them to do or perform[20]. A task is an assignment allocated by the teacher that has a purpose. Whether your students with dyslexia are using their worksheets or workbooks, conducting their scientific project with their colleagues or writing an essay paper for you, there is always a purpose of the task you have asked them to do. The more you explain the rationale behind the task the better it is for your students' information processing abilities. Their focus and attention span and their cognitive efforts and overall learning will benefit if you clearly explain the rationale behind the task you are asking your students with dyslexia to do. There is nothing more boring than a teacher telling students to open their book on a certain page and asking them to do a certain exercise without explaining why or how is that relevant to what they are learning. Teachers need to explain why it is important for their students with dyslexia to do this exercise, and what they are going to accomplish by doing it. Always explain and provide your rationale behind doing tasks because they make your tasks more important and it provides relevance to the learning situation as well as continuity. It provides a relationship also to the learned content as the task will be seen as a continuation of learning and not separate from it.

Explain your reasoning for asking to complete certain tasks in order to assist your students with dyslexia making connections between the procedure at hand and the underlying conceptual knowledge. Different students with dyslexia work differently, so explain why you are doing what you are doing now and explain to them how important such a task is for their learning. Doing this will give them purpose and will allow them time to reflect on what they have just learned. It will also implicitly teach them that every new learned content or material needs to be practised on by tasks and that practise makes perfect. Self-explaining establishes connections between conceptual and procedural knowledge.

Such connections contextualise their knowledge by providing your students with dyslexia the why and when of learning and therefore makes the material easier to remember. Self-explaining is an excellent tool for students with dyslexia when they learn new concepts. Your rationale may include reasons for the choice and design of task, and it can also contain what your students with dyslexia will get out of it and why they should undertake it in a particular way. Teachers' rationale for tasks that are common and usual, such as essays and exams, may need particularly careful thought.

Use an appropriate task difficulty level

Vygotsky's instrumental work was explained in his Theory of Social Development (1978) in which he argued that learning assists students in their own development and that students' cognitive development originates from social interactions facilitated by guided learning, i.e., teaching, within the zone of proximal development[21]. The Zone of Proximal Development is a central concept in Vygotsky's theory as students and their teachers or classmates co-construct knowledge. Vygotsky explained that if the task is too difficult, students will feel frustrated and if the task is too easy, students will feel bored. Learning does not take place in any of those situations. Learning occurs in the zone of proximal development when the task difficulty level is appropriate to the readiness level of students taking into account their cognitive abilities. For Vygotsky, the environment in which students interact with, and notably their classroom, will influence how they think and what they think about. In addition to the classroom environment, the task difficulty level will also affect learning and teachers are advised to ensure that such a task difficulty level is appropriate to the current level of the student because it has a big effect on their motivation.

Task difficulty refers to work assignments that exceed the skill level of students with dyslexia. It is important for teachers to know and determine which aspects of the task do not match their students' abilities and how they can adjust it to increase chances of success in completing the task[22]. Assignments that are too difficult for students with dyslexia or require them to use skill sets that are challenging may result in problem behaviour while providing tasks at the correct level of difficulty promotes on-task behaviour and task completion[23].

Similarly, decreasing the task length and allowing frequent breaks will assist in decreasing problem behaviour[24]. The task difficulty of assignments in a classroom influences the level of student motivation by influencing whether or not there is an expectancy of success and the level of effort put forth[25]. It can influence self-efficacy and the level and amount of information learned[26]. Although such influences affect all learners, they tend to have particular importance for students with dyslexia[27].

Utilise social media

Social media has become a regular part of our students' lives. They use it widely to communicate with their friends or to share their photos and post their status updates on a regular basis. Facebook, Instagram, Pinterest, Twitter, YouTube and Snapchat are all very well known to most students now. Part of their popularity is the fact that they are easily installed on students' smart phones instead of desktops or laptops only. This technology has changed the way students learn. Teachers should adapt their teaching methods to these new expectations. Break your lessons up into more easily digestible sections and use digital applications whenever appropriate. This may particularly work better with your high school students than traditional teaching methods. If you are not sure how to adapt to such technology, ask your students with dyslexia to show you and get their input on ways to make the class more engaging and learning more fun. Instead of asking your students with dyslexia to put away their phones, especially in situations when it is very hard or challenging to do so, try to think of novel ways where such social media tools can be utilised to enhance learning. This will help make learning more relevant and fun for your students.

You can utilise Twitter to encourage your students to conduct research. Your students can identify three recent tweets regarding the topic you are about to explain in your history class. You can task your students with creating a Facebook page for the historical figure they are studying now. They will collect necessary information, build the page, register it and upload photos and write comments. This is informative, and materials learned will be easily remembered because it is fun and on Facebook! For students with dyslexia, social media is used to chat with friends and share photos, but they can do a classroom account and benefit from it in their education and school[28]. Such groups can also be used to share homework, give test reminders, and create a classroom community. Obviously this has to be done if the rules of your educational institution allows it and if it is done professionally with respect to privacy and appropriate codes of acceptable behaviour. However, if you or your students with dyslexia do not prefer or are not ready to fully use social media in the classroom, use tools that have similar collaboration features. Whooo's Reading[29] is sometimes referred to as the 'Facebook for reading' because it has many similar features of Facebook including comments and likes. Google Docs© allows students to collaborate and comment in real-time, similar to Facebook. Diigo© is another useful web platform which allows students to tag websites, create a personal library, share with their classmates and structure their research[30].

Utilise scaffolding techniques

Scaffolding is breaking up the learning into chunks and providing a structure with each chunk. The term refers to supports that are built into the task to develop an understanding of it. The supports are then withdrawn gradually, when the learner has achieved the necessary understanding to continue with less support until they can independently perform the tasks on their own. The metaphor of scaffolding is derived from construction work where it represents a temporary structure that is used to erect a building. In the field of education and instruction, scaffolding refers to support that is specific and tailored to students' needs. Teachers always have a role in supporting their students' development and providing support structures to get them to that next level and they use various scaffolding techniques to do so. However, it is important to note that scaffolding has a temporary effect and it lasts only until students with dyslexia master a particular skill. After that, the scaffold gradually disappears. With scaffolding, students with dyslexia should be able to master the concept and complete related tasks independently. Scaffolding provides special assistance so that learners can move on to learn new skills and concepts. The goal of scaffolding techniques is to help students with dyslexia become independent and self-regulated learners. With scaffolding, learners are encouraged to become more active and engaged in the learning process which will develop their critical-thinking skills.

Teachers use many types of scaffolding techniques which tend to depend on the types of activities performed during a given class. Breaking tasks into smaller, more manageable parts is a good scaffolding technique. Teachers can also use a 'think aloud' or 'verbalise your thinking' process when encouraging their students with dyslexia to complete a task. Cooperative learning is yet another good scaffolding approach. The important point to consider for teachers is that they have to be mindful of keeping their students with dyslexia in pursuit of the task while minimising their stress level. Tasks that are too far out of reach for students with dyslexia lead to frustration while tasks that are too easy cause boredom. Providing more support than the student needs at the beginning of the task can be motivating so long as these are gradually removed. When scaffolding reading, for example, teachers may preview the text and discuss key vocabulary, or chunk the text and then read and discuss as they go. Scaffolding is an instructional technique whereby teachers model the desired learning strategy or task and then gradually shifts responsibility to the students with dyslexia.

Utilise appropriate assessment methods

To keep up with the ever-changing needs of their students and to effectively inform their instruction, teachers are encouraged to use a variety of assessment tools. Traditional forms of assessment have been used to determine student progress and assign grades. Although traditional forms of assessment have value, if they are designed poorly or misused, they can negatively affect student motivation. There are two important points through which assessment can have an impact on students' motivation[31]. Assessment can increase motivation through providing an incentive or could apply pressure to lower motivation. While some researchers claim that more frequent tests increase students' motivation, others view online assessments to increase motivation[32]. Assessment impacts students differently and it is beneficial if assessments can be adapted to fit the student. A flexible assessment system can be more effective in increasing motivation.

Teachers should try to think of assessments that are enjoyable to take or the ones that are intrinsically motivating. Some assessments provide clear tangible extrinsic goals to students with dyslexia such as: Grade promotion or graduation. Other assessments provide extrinsic goals to teachers themselves or schools because they are used for their accountability purposes. Pressures arising from assessments can affect students with dyslexia negatively. Assessments that include short-term goals which are easily achievable and which gradually increase in their level of difficulty can potentially build students' confidence. Assessments that allow students with dyslexia to understand ahead of time what they will be tested on can assist them by giving them clear knowledge of what is expected of them. If the assessment practices utilised by teachers help students with dyslexia feel learning is an interesting and enjoyable process, students are more likely to be intrinsically motivated. If the assessment practices utilised by teachers make students feel their learning is an important process for self-improvement, students with dyslexia may possess the self-determined extrinsic motivation to learn.

Linking assessments to real life scenarios are great for students with dyslexia. If your assessment involves a writing assignment for instance, ask your students to analyse an excellent writing assignment and a poor one. Do not tell them yourself, but ask your students with dyslexia to iden-tify what makes the good example strong and the poor example weak. This will encourage them to practise analytical skills and form their own arguments rather than just repeating information.

Utilise extracurricular activities

Some students with dyslexia respond better when they are being motivated in non-academic contexts, particularly those who are good athletes or good at problem solving or creative. Creating an environment in which those students can feel interconnected and socially accepted will no doubt support and increase their feelings of relatedness which in turns increase their level of motivation. Students with dyslexia who participate in extracurricular activities tend to learn new skills that can probably assist them to become competent in the classroom. School extracurricular activities have a positive impact on school engagement, participation and achievement[33]. Dropout rate of students was also sig-nificantly reduced for students with dyslexia who had participated in extracurricular activities. Such connections between the two have also been shown in school attendance, school engagement and participation[34]. They have also been linked to stronger social relationships and better self-esteem[35]. After-school activities specially for students with dyslexia from lower income families have the potential to provide them with experiences that are otherwise only accessible for students from middle and upper class families. It is by participating in such extracurricular activities that students with dyslexia increase their sense of relatedness, interest and competence which in turn improves their academic motiv-ation and success.

After-school activities which include art and music can be used as rewards to encourage participation in the learning process if students with dyslexia like to take part in them. However, after-school activities like art and music can also be used to boost learning if collaboration between those who provide them and the students' teacher are organised. Learning content can be reinforced and repeated through after-school activities without students with dyslexia even realising that they are doing it. Take art for instance, they could be asked about a journey to the beach and to draw it, then, the following day, the teacher during the school day asks them to write an essay about a journey to the beach. I call this integrated learning and I found it to be extremely useful for students with dyslexia. Teachers are advised to collaborate among themselves and share their learning objectives to cement learning through introducing the content in similar lessons and via different activities and modalities. Students with dyslexia can for instance discuss creativity in their after-school music sessions and explore how a famous musician was creative only to then be asked to write an essay about creativity in their literacy lesson the following day. It is these examples that I think teachers can utilise to increase the motivation of their students with dyslexia.

Explain long-term benefits

'When am I ever going to need to know this?' is all too familiar a sentence for some teachers, especially those teaching middle and high school students when they are learning about a subject matter that they perceive not important or not relevant or not interesting. When students with dyslexia fail to understand the long-term benefits of the work they are doing at school, they become unmotivated. The term 'domain specific motivation' refers to students' specific motivation to study or know about certain subjects only that they prefer to study or engage in all the time because of their personal interests and current learning and life experiences. Domain specificity of motivation increases with age. Domain specific motivation increases when students grow and gain more educational experiences and when their curriculum starts to reflect departmentalisation of academic subjects[36].

Students with dyslexia attach more value to activities that they excel in overtime and those students will be more motivated to learn the subjects they experience success in[37]. Other subjects that do not interest them and do not attract their attention gets neglected and ignored. That is why teachers should explain the connections between their subject matter and the course material they are teaching and the 'real world'. Clarifying such connections makes learning beneficial and relevant to students with dyslexia. It also ensures that long-term benefits of what the students are actually learning are known to them.

I heard one of my teachers once giving me a real-life example concerning one of his previous students who did not enjoy chemistry and who was not keen to know about it at all. All that particular student cared about was maths and he could have studied maths all day long. Whenever a chemistry class came, he would always say: How on earth am I going to benefit from this? My teacher told us that fate has it that years later, he met the same student and by that time he had already graduated and studied finance. The student ended up working as an accountant in a pharmaceutical company that produces the same chemicals that the student was not keen to learn about in his chemistry class. Because of this, he was not strong in chemistry and was not able to be promoted faster in his company or travel and attend important business meetings regarding his company's expansion because another accountant in the company was good in maths and also good in chemistry. Refusing to pay attention to his chemistry classes based on the fact that he might not ever benefit from it in his life has affected that particular student negatively. This is a real life example, so use it, or use your own examples if you know of some, to explain to your students with dyslexia how what they learn at school benefits them not only in their school exams and grades but also later in their real life situations.

Encourage collaboration

Cooperative learning is a learning approach where students work together in small groups to achieve a group goal. By working in small groups, students realise that their rewards are dependent on the success of their team members and as such are encouraged to provide support for each other's learning. Such collaboration is very important in the classroom and notably in the case of students who are struggling. Students with dyslexia can achieve success when they are paired with another student who can assist them (study buddy)[38]. Use of collaborative and cooperative learning tends to strengthen students' motivation[39]. Motivation is indeed one of the potential catalysts through which cooperative learning affects achievement[40]. Peer encouragement and support tends to improve task engagement and the learning situations in the case of collaborative learning methods tend to draw students' attention to the tasks more than traditional teaching methods[41]. Students work in groups to accomplish a particular learning objective[42]. For such a cooperative learning model to work, there must be two conditions: First, there must be group goals or what is sometimes referred to as positive interdependence. Second, there must still be individual accountability. The group will depend on its individual members' ability to learn for the sake of all its group members. Both conditions, i.e., positive interdependence and individual accountability, develop an overall feeling that each member is important to the group.

While traditional teaching methods use competition to motivate students, cooperative learning approaches utilise cooperation strategies instead to motivate students with dyslexia. The impact of peer support for learning is great in cooperative learning methods and it is welcomed by peers and felt by everyone in the group. Cooperative learning enhances students' self-esteem, which in turn motivates more students to participate. It is through helping one another, that students with dyslexia can build a supportive community in order to raise the performance of all its members. Cooperative learning increases student motivation by allowing them more control over their own learning experiences. It also gives groups ownership of their learning. Lines of communication are opened during cooperative learning sessions while students with dyslexia are actively encouraged to explain their actions and thoughts to each other and to their teacher.

Encourage learning styles

Every student has learning preferences and styles that are best suited to their way of learning. While some students have a dominant learning style, others prefer to learn using a mix of them. There is no right or wrong learning style. Teachers should help their students with dyslexia discover their preferred learning styles. Discovering your students' preferred learning style and appealing to them will improve the rate and quality of your students' learning. Students with dyslexia can be visual, auditory or physical learners. Others may be more logical in their style or social while some may prefer learning on their own. Students with dyslexia who are visual prefer learning by seeing how things work while students with dyslexia who are auditory would rather learn best by listening to things being explained. Explore your students' learning preferences and employ different types of learnings styles to maximise their learning. The assessment of learning styles can help teachers develop teaching strategies and can be used to increase the effectiveness of the group activities.

Learning styles can change over time as they adapt to changing circumstances and new cognitive experiences. Learning styles provide information about your students' skills and learning abilities and therefore assist teachers in optimising the effectiveness of their teaching activities. Teachers can consult many tools that are readily available to find the suitable learning styles of their students. While some of those tools are electronic, others are pen and paper. Some are free and group based, while others are not and generate nice looking graphs and come with their pre-prepared recommendations. While learning styles are popular among many teachers, some researchers have questioned their scientific validity. Regardless of the views about learning styles and their uses, rest assured that as a teacher, you can train your students with dyslexia to improve the areas of their learning that are letting them down by simply using them more. If they feel that they are not confident learning visually, get them into the habit of reading the charts and diagrams in an article before focusing on the ideas in the text. Learning styles allow teachers to examine the strengths and weaknesses in their cognitive profile of their students with dyslexia which in turn would allow them to make the most of any aspects of learning that come naturally to their students. Teachers should do everything they can to gain a rounded picture of their students' learning. Teachers should reflect on and consider all the different reasons why their students with dyslexia tend to approach learning the way you do. Encourage your students with dyslexia to ask themselves while learning: Why I am doing this in that particular way? Is this the most effective for me? Or is it because it is the way I have always done it before?

Encourage active involvement

A classroom full of active and responsive students is very rewarding for teachers because active participation from the part of students adds quality and depth to the learning process. Getting students to contribute to the learning process inside the classroom requires planning and creativity. Active involvement in the classroom occurs when students get to move and engage in classroom learning activities. The goal of increasing participation and active involvement in the classroom is not to have every student participate in the same way or at the same rate, but to create an environment in which all students have the opportunity to learn. The essence of active involvement is to develop activities where students need to actively use their brain to participate. Students with an interest in a particular subject tend to pay more attention to it and work on it to a level greater than the average one. Their engagement is high, with respectively higher quality of learning.

The use of prompts utilises students' inquisitive nature and encourages their active engagement, so use them. Verbal and visual prompts can be introduced at different points during the lesson to introduce a topic or to relate to a background knowledge. They can also be used to review information at the end of the lesson. Set out a name jar and put inside it all of your students' names. When asking questions, the jar is passed around the class, and students can pull out a name for each question. The named person has to answer the question and then pull out the next name for the next question. This activity increases students' attention in the classroom. Many students with dyslexia who frequently volunteer to contribute inside the classroom are active learners who typically tend to think while they are actually speaking. Create conditions that enable students of various learning preferences and personalities to contribute inside your classroom. To reach this goal, take extra steps to encourage quiet students to speak up and ask students who tend to be more involved to actually hold back from commenting in order to give their other classmates a chance. Initiate discussions whenever possible as students with dyslexia will open up and contribute more than merely listening all the time. Link your lesson to real life scenarios to make them more interesting for your students. Have all the students stand up inside your class, and either randomly or in an order have students voice out one point that they learned before they sit down. You can increase difficulty of your questions gradually. Ensure that your students with dyslexia understand that this is a learning activity and therefore wrong answers are OK so long as your students are trying and making an effort to participate.

Encourage self-questioning

Questions are excellent tools at our disposal that we can utilise to point us in the right direction. Questions can help us find direction, purpose and the best approach towards resolving a problem or finding motivation[43]. Each one of us has our own triggers that can help us identify our motivation. Our students with dyslexia are no different. That is why as a teacher it is very important for you to train your students with dyslexia to ask themselves questions and to find out what works best for them. This includes questions like: Have they done this before? What were their reasons for wanting to achieve their goal? How did they do it? Is this the best way to tackle this problem? This can also be motivating as again the lead role is coming from the students and this can be reinforcing and it does lead to control over learning. Teach your students with dyslexia to take a step back and think about what makes their goal important to them. It is important to remind your students about what matters to them. Their values are a big part of their motivators, so by teaching them to explore their values, they will be able to tap into their motivation.

Big long goals are overwhelming and decrease motivation. Breaking goals into small, manageable steps can help students focus and take small actions to achieve them. Progression through their goals and seeing the results greatly boost their motivation.

Self-questioning enables students with dyslexia to ask relevant questions on how to break the goals into small bits and what necessary steps to take to achieve them[44]. What would be the consequences of not being motivated to achieve their goal? Some of your students with dyslexia will be more motivated by finding the answer to this question as they would be worried about the negative impact of not achieving their goals rather than the positive benefits of achieving it. The more aware your students with dyslexia are of what it is they need to change, the easier it is for them to take action to make such changes. Students with dyslexia specially those who have experienced instances of repeated failure may develop limiting beliefs and it is those limiting beliefs that sabotage their motivation. Therefore, train them to identify the barriers that they may face or the ones that may sabotage their motivation. By encouraging your students with dyslexia to ask those questions, they would recognise those obstacles and try to deal with them one by one. What habits can your students with dyslexia create to increase their motivation? What practical reminders do they need to put in place to motivate them? Who among their close circle of friends or family members can they reach out to in order to increase their motivation? How are your students with dyslexia going to reward themselves? Who will reward them once they achieve what they seek? Train your students to ask themselves all of those questions.

Encourage self-motivation

Self-motivation is the process of applying positive thought patterns and certain belief structures in order to optimise or sustain engagement in learning. Being self-motivated is a critical skill for school and life in general. It is a fundamental part of achieving goals and feeling fulfilled. An important role of teachers is to raise the level of awareness of their students concerning self-regulatory strategies and how to apply them to promote themselves[45]. Engaging in motivational thinking is indeed motivational itself for the individual and it involves taking personal control of the affective conditions and experiences necessary for learning. Dörnyei (2001) has classified self-motivating strategies into five main categories[46]:

1   *Commitment control strategies*: Which are those who assist in preserving or increasing the learner's original goal commitment (such as focusing on what would happen if the original goal was not realised).
2   *Metacognitive control strategies*: Which are those strategies utilised to monitor and control concentration (such as identifying distractions and keeping them under control).
3   *Situation control strategies*: Which are those strategies used to decrease boredom and adding attraction to the task (such as using one's fantasy to make the task more entertaining).
4   *Emotion control strategies*: Which are those strategies used to manage disruptive emotional states or moods (such as self-encouragement and using relaxation techniques).
5   *Environmental control strategies*: Which are those strategies used to eliminate negative environmental influences (such as eliminating distractions).

Allowing your students with dyslexia choices in their learning and assisting them in setting their own goals are great self-motivators for them. Self-motivation comes from intrinsic motivation so focus on this aspect of their motivation. Teachers are also encouraged to ensure that they understand that most of the ideas presented until now will really assist them in increasing their self-motivation.

Encourage self-assessment

Self-assessment is the process whereby students monitor and evaluate the quality of their thinking and learning and identify strategies that improve their understanding. Self-assessment occurs when students judge their own work to improve performance as they identify discrepancies between current and desired performance. Self-assessment is a major component of learning because students gather information and reflect on their own learning[47]. It enhances the process of transferring students into lifelong learners. Providing students with dyslexia with some tips for self-assessment is not only a good learning tool but can be motivating as students will have control over their own learning. Self-assessment is a valuable learning tool as through self-assessment, students with dyslexia can identify their own skill gaps, identify where to focus their learning, review their own work, re-adjust their goals to more realistic ones and finally decide when and how to move to the next level.

Self-assessment can increase the interest and motivation of students with dyslexia for subjects at hand which will lead to an overall enhanced learning experience and a better academic performance. This process helps students stay involved and motivated and encourages self-reflection and responsibility for their own learning. Teachers are advised to train their students with dyslexia on self-assessment criteria and how to apply them in grading their work. Teachers can also give their students with dyslexia practice sessions assessing their own work. Self-assessment can also be tried with peer assessment. Self-assessment as a process involves three subcomponents: Self-monitoring, self-evaluation and the implementation of corrective actions for enhanced learning. In a typical self-assessment process, students with dyslexia are expected to identify their own learning and performance strategies, come up with feedback for themselves based on pre-defined criteria with their teacher and finally determining the next plan of action to improve their performance. Students with dyslexia who practise self-assessment more tend to pay more attention to what they are doing. Those students are also better judges of their own progress and they tend to be better at identifying what is needed to achieve their desired level of mastery or skill.

Do not over test

Quality assessments generate good data which can provide much needed and valuable information regarding students' progress for teachers. Such good data distilled from assessment and testing have the potential to support accountability and promote high quality teaching and learning. Testing as a part of an ongoing assessment and monitoring of progress is essential and vital for the learning process. Over testing is not. Although tests and quizzes are effective ways to better estimate our students' understanding level, they can also add unnecessary stress on them. For students with dyslexia, testing places an emotional burden on them which they experience in the form of anxiety and stress. The number of tests and the time devoted to tests should therefore be limited to the minimum. Tests and preparation for them should not take precedence over good quality learning. Testing should be conducted to aid learning and facilitate learning not to hinder it. Tests do not necessarily provide an estimation for the understanding level of every student with dyslexia because some students do well during tests. Other students for example will respond better to and feel more comfortable in discussions. Also, tests that are composed mostly of multiple-choice questions would not assess students' ability to come up with their own answers. In some situations, test preparation becomes the instruction, i.e., with instructional materials and exercises all directed to prepare for the tests rather than learning.

There are so many reasons why over testing takes place. Tests and assessments are somehow inexpensive when compared with recommended changes that involve increasing instructional time or reducing a classroom size. Testing and assessments can also be externally mandated, rapidly implemented and their results are visible and tangible. In the case of students with dyslexia where they have to be moved from one tier to another, many tests have to be conducted before such a movement can take place and before they are eligible for additional literacy and numeracy provisions. Such a situation of eligibility has a knock-on effect for their morale and self-esteem because they have to be over tested in subjects that they are having challenges with which adds to their predicament. So teachers are advised to watch out and avoid over testing because it is very demotivating for students with dyslexia.

Motivate through type of test used

Assessment is an information gathering process. It refers to any activity that is focusing on collecting data evidence that is planned, systematic and aimed at evaluating and judging learning. There are various types of assessments that can be classified according to various factors involved in the assessment process. One way of classifying assessments is according to its purpose. If the purpose of assessment is to help in decisions about how to advance learning, the assessment is considered formative but if the purpose of assessment is to summarise learning covered so far to grade and produce certificates, then the assessment is considered summative. Assessments can also be criterion referenced or norm referenced according to their benchmarks. Criterion-referenced tests use preapproved benchmarks to evaluate students' learning such as the curriculum for instance. Norm-referenced tests use norms as the benchmark to evaluate students' learning. Norms tend to be collected from large groups of students in a fair, systematic and standardised manner.

Teachers may use their own quizzes to test their students with dyslexia or perhaps build their own teacher-based tests to evaluate progress. Different tests used in the assessment process affect motivation differently. While criterion-referenced tests use comparisons that tend to support motivation, normative-referenced tests use comparisons that decrease motivation[48]. Most assessments strongly encourage achieving performance goals rather than mastery goals and therefore it is not surprising that students with dyslexia tend to feel anxious or frustrated during assessments. As a teacher, you are always advised to look at performance growth not only performance levels when you are interpreting assessment results. Challenging tasks will only stimulate intrinsic motivation to continue *if* threat of external evaluation is minimised.

The more information is provided during the evaluation process, the less likely it will be viewed by the student as controlling. Teachers' own class-testing practices can help increase the self-efficacy of their students, if they explain well the purpose and expectations of their tests and if they provide accurate and frequent feedback. Constructive discussion of testing and the development of desirable assessment practice in the school as a whole has a positive effect on learning as opposed to only focusing on performance outcomes which tend to have a negative effect on learning. You are advised therefore as a teacher to present assessment realistically, not as an end product in itself but a process that is inherently not 100% accurate (we call this an inherent level of analysis), and that promotes reflection for learning and is indicative of learning and not definitive.

Notes

1   Trussell, 2008.
2   Baines et al., 2003.
3   Rands & Gansemer-Topf, 2017.
4   McKeown et al., 2015.
5   Van den Berg et al., 2012.

 6 Gest & Rodkin, 2011.
 7 Harvey & Kenyon, 2013.
 8 Gottfried, 2009.
 9 Britt, 2005.
10 Spence et al., 2006.
11 lifehacker.com.
12 Webb, 1989.
13 Sencibaugh & Sencibaugh, 2016.
14 Clifford, 1972.
15 Ryan et al., 2015.
16 Hamilton et al., 2009.
17 Wayman, 2005.
18 Wohlstetter et al., 2008.
19 Maynard & Hakel, 1997.
20 Shaklee, 1976.
21 Vygotsky, 1978.
22 Scott et al., 2012.
23 Kern & Clemens, 2007.
24 Dunlap et al., 1991.
25 Hom & Maxwell, 1983.
26 Li et al., 2007.
27 Margolis & McCabe, 2004.
28 Wilson & Boldeman, 2012.
29 www.whooosreading.org.
30 www.diigo.com.
31 Elikai & Schuhmann, 2010.
32 Pachran et al., 2013.
33 Melnick & Sabo, 1992.
34 Shulruf, 2010.
35 Marsh & Kleitman, 2003.
36 Gottfried et al., 2001.
37 Eccles & Wigfield, 2002.
38 Roe et al., 2005.
39 Turner, 1995.
40 Hidi & Harackiewicz, 2000.
41 Guthrie et al., 2000.
42 Stipek, 1996.
43 Park & Crocker, 2013.
44 Schuitema et al., 2012.
45 Pintrich & DeGroot, 1990.
46 Dörnyei, 2001.
47 Shimabukuro et al., 1999.
48 Stipek, 1996.

9   Motivate students with dyslexia
    by developing your personal
    qualities

Embrace change

As an effective teacher, you have the opportunity to push for and model change for your students[1]. If you are innovative in the classroom, your students are more likely to become adaptable and innovative learners and such skills will serve them well. We should not expect our students to be innovative unless we are first willing to be innovative ourselves. Some students with dyslexia resist change because they believe it will not matter anyway. However, your efforts as a teacher to embrace change will create better learning opportunities for your students. Believe in your ability to use change to make a positive impact on them. Be flexible and go with the flow when change occurs. Do not complain about changes when a new principal arrives or a new textbook is used. Do not feel the need to mention how good you had it at your last school or with your last group of students compared to your current circumstances now. Instead of stressing about change, embrace it with your hands wide open. It is not in fact productive to resist change, because it is impossible to avoid it. Change will happen. When you embrace it, you can influence its direction and outcomes. So, change can either happen to you, or you can take ownership of it. Most of us become comfortable with things the way they are, even though everything around us may be changing. The only way we can provide schooling that is relevant is to accept change and learn and grow.

Effective teachers cannot grow without risking something. We as humans tend to stay with what is familiar because we are comfortable with it. However, what is familiar is not necessarily progress. Instead, train your students with dyslexia to have a growth mindset. It is OK to take risks and try new things that we are not sure about sometimes. If we fail, it will not be fatal; but rather it will be a proof that we are trying. Some teachers resist change because of their personal preferences. Even if they see that an idea has the potential to improve things for their students and learning, they may not embrace it because it makes them uncomfortable. Educators cannot afford this mindset. Be flexible and welcome any opportunity that can move education forward. It can be very difficult to put aside the things that we find most comfortable. But when you step out of your comfort zone, there is potential for incredible fulfilment and reward. We stand to gain so much for our students and for our own personal fulfilment. Innovation and change start with a belief that there might be a better way. We have to believe these opportunities await.

Be organised

Most students respond positively to a well-organised subject taught by an enthusiastic teacher who has a real interest in his students and what they learn. Brewer and colleagues (2001) found that highly structured, well organised and outcomes oriented teachers seem to maintain student motivation[2]. A teacher's ability to organise themself and their classroom materials and schedules greatly increases the teacher–student relationship and learning efficacy. This is particularly important within the first few weeks of each school year as both classroom expectations and behaviour can be set right from the start. Classroom management depends on a teacher's early organisation skills, which in turn leads to student cooperation, engagement and productivity.

Helping your students organise their papers, books and assignments will go a long way to helping them feel motivated to learn. Disorganisation is typical among young school age children, but it can also lead to a feeling of being overwhelmed. Overwhelmed children lose time and effort feeling frustrated and worried instead of focusing on their own learning. Be patient, but consistent, in helping your students with dyslexia organise their school supplies and assignments. This will help them feel in control, less overwhelmed and more motivated to learn.

Keep a central filing system on your desk or on top of everyday classroom instructions. Use baskets, crates or standard cardboard file boxes that are strong and have mobile holders for important daily material such as calendars, handouts, forms, progress reports and reward stickers. Use a storage cabinet if possible and locate it near your desk to keep essential and often used supplies such as sentence strips, student folders and large items. Keep other useful storage items such as zip-lock bags and small plastic containers near you and ready to use at any time. These can be used to organise papers, books and manipulatives. Some students with dyslexia lack structure and tend to lose their space and their place. It helps a great deal if you yourself are organised and structured as you can assist them organising themselves. Not only should they be organised in their personal belongings and materials but also in their own thinking, time management skills and in their study habits too. Organised teachers can help their students with dyslexia become organised, which will in turn boost their achievement and motivation.

Structure your lesson

Good lesson planning is an essential component of teaching and learning. The effective teacher is always well prepared and enjoys a successful instructional experience with his students. The development of interesting lessons and in particular how well structured they are should take a great amount of time, thought and effort from teachers. To become an effective teacher, you must be committed to spending the required necessary time to prepare your lesson well and in particular how it is structured and paced.

Structure your lesson in such a way that important bits of information are always highlighted. Good teaching habits dictate that a short brief introduction about what was learned last session/lesson is always advisable. Information linked in chains or related to each other are easier to remember than fragmented ones. Always start your lesson with a brief summary of last knowledge learned or covered and then gently prepare your students with dyslexia for the new information being introduced. This is a good way to structure your lessons and always remember to include plenty of time for explanation, working in groups, doing exercises, discussions and some independent work. Consistency is very important if you are trying to build a structure for your lessons.

A clearly thought out lesson has its own structure or a set of steps that need to be achieved or covered as well as parts in between to be filled with knowledge through scaffolding. A thorough lesson plan should inspire students while at the same time helps the teacher to evaluate their teaching and compare it with the previously set objectives. Lesson plans develop self-confidence in teachers and makes them work towards a definite goal. They have enough thought in them towards time taken to cover each learning objective as well as enough material to cover all aspects of the learning situation. A well-structured lesson involves the teacher taking proper care by considering both the current level and the previous knowledge of all the students in their class including students with dyslexia. A well-structured lesson is motivating because many students with dyslexia lack structure themselves and if lessons are well structured, it helps reassure them that they are already familiar with what is coming next because they are familiar with the actual structure of the lesson itself. A structured lesson is a well-timed lesson where each element is given its due time according to its importance and level of difficulty.

Use different types of teaching

Because different students learn differently, it is universally accepted among teachers that more than one way of teaching is recommended if you are aiming to become an effective teacher. Using different methods of teaching appeals to different students, increases engagement and facilitates information retention as it captures your students' attention and curiosity. Highly achieving students tend to benefit from teaching methods that are less rigid and more flexible. Students with low conceptual levels tend to benefit from highly organised environments[3]. It is well understood that no teaching strategy will consistently engage all learners. Instead, help your students with dyslexia relate the learning content to their own previous backgrounds and their prior knowledge while understanding new concepts. Regardless of your chosen method of teaching, always maintain eye contact at all times with your students and move toward them when you interact with them. You can gently move your head to signal that you are listening to them. Encourage them to share their ideas and comments, even if they are incorrect. Also, teachers will never know what their students with dyslexia do not understand unless they ask them. Give frequent positive feedback that supports your students' beliefs and empower them to do well. Ensure opportunities for students' success by assigning tasks with an appropriate level of difficulty. Help your students with dyslexia find personal meaning and value in the material they are studying, and help them feel that they are valued members of the learning community inside and outside the classroom.

Teachers need to vary their teaching styles and techniques in order not to cause boredom to their students inside the classroom[4]. Effective teachers always seek greater insight into how their students with dyslexia learn from and the effect of their own discussion and interaction with their students and the way they handle the lesson in the classroom. Identify the points of strengths and weaknesses in your students with dyslexia and start your teaching methods according to their points of strengths as it is the effective choice you can make. Students' interests contribute to learning, so use this fact when you are planning your preferred teaching method.

Be open-minded

An open-minded teacher is the one who is willing to consider the collective experiences, beliefs, opinions, values and perspectives that are different from his own. An open-minded teacher is the one who allows his students to actually experience how different and diverse people around the world think and behave. Open-mindedness is really important in teaching students with dyslexia to understand how contextual factors affect and indeed shape the way people in their own circles think and operate. Teachers who were open minded, friendly, enthusiastic and knowledgeable about student' names and interests were found to motivate their students the most[5]. Teachers' out-of-classroom rapport with students is also an important factor in motivating students. Do not feel bitter with your students with dyslexia when they have an opinion about your teaching. Instead, be open-minded and develop your ability to receive constructive criticism and form a plan of action. On the other hand, one of the deadly sins for a teacher to commit is to give students with dyslexia a sense that they are not being respected. The class will probably be a bad experience for everyone no matter what else you do. If a teacher clearly conveys open-mindedness, friendliness, respect and caring, it will cover a multitude of pedagogical sins a teacher may commit.

Being friendly with your students with dyslexia can give their personality a nice push as they tend to feel restricted in an unfriendly classroom setting. A friendly teacher makes his students with dyslexia feel at ease especially in the case of younger ones. Also, when students perceive the teacher to be friendly, they are more encouraged to engage in open discussions without feeling subdued. Friendly teachers have the ability to develop healthy learning and teaching relationships with their students with dyslexia faster and such relationships tend to last longer. Feedback given by a friendly teacher is always perceived as constructive and given with care which in turn supports the learning process. The case is more important among young learners who feel slightly more vulnerable when receiving feedback from the teacher and would feel really upset if they receive strong criticism in front of the whole classroom.

Be approachable

Being approachable is a pre-requite for student engagement which in turn fuels student motivation. Students with dyslexia do not engage fully in learning experiences with teachers whom they perceive to be unapproachable. Dealing with very young learners can be tricky, so if you are approachable, your job as a teacher will be much easier for you and more rewarding for your students. Be approachable in order for students with dyslexia to feel comfortable enough to come to you with their issues or concerns. By being more approachable as a teacher, your students with dyslexia are more likely to ask you questions which opens lines of communication in the classroom. Also, by being more approachable, you show your students with dyslexia that you are indeed passionate about what you are teaching them and how they learn from your lessons. Once this happens, students with dyslexia in return feel more committed to their programme of study and this ultimately leads them to attain better grades.

For a young learner, teachers can be intimidating sometimes. While all students are sitting, there they stand and what a powerful situation that is. While all students are silent inside the classroom listening with intent, teachers are the only one speaking and is also in control of who else is allowed to speak. Teachers decide the pace of the lesson, which day the quiz or the exam is going to be and which grade to assign to their students when they mark their papers. With this much power inside the classroom and over learners, teachers must work equally hard to become approachable. For their students with dyslexia, feeling comfortable with a person who has these responsibilities can be hard. Teachers have the ability and the responsibility to make such a process easier. Use time before and after class to chat with your students with dyslexia and allow opportunities to share experiences. Throw in a few jokes and use humour. Teach your students with dyslexia that it's ok to make mistakes sometimes and that they are in a comfortable and supportive place.

If you view teaching as an opportunity for dialogue between you and your students, they will be more engaged and they will find you approachable. Being approachable depends on your ability to get to know your students, your enthusiasm for teaching and your ability to display humour and your humility. When students with dyslexia feel that their teachers are open and approachable, they believe that nothing they have to say is ridiculous. In this case, students with dyslexia will feel more comfortable to let you know when they are feeling uninspired. In such situations, consider it a challenge for you as a teacher to find a way to motivate your students with dyslexia. You do not need to act as a therapist to each and every student. However, students know and feel for teachers who are perceived to be caring and approachable. Do not force your students with dyslexia to tell you why they are feeling uninspired. Instead, let them come to you about such issues by focusing on being approachable.

Be caring

Great teachers care about their students. They want them to succeed and are committed to helping them achieve their goals. Teachers also care about their students' happiness, well-being and life beyond the class-room. Be a great teacher and do not make it a secret that you care. Go that extra mile and motivate your students with dyslexia by encouraging them, rewarding them and incentivising them. Getting involved in this manner shows your students with dyslexia that you are vested in their education. If you do the best job you can to teach your students, for sure they will notice. Meet with your students' parents during teacher parent conferences and school functions. Send notes home about your students' performance. Ask them how things are outside the classroom. Celebrate their birthdays in a small but special way. Make your students with dyslexia feel as if their life and not just their homework, grades and attendance is of interest to you.

When teachers care about their students with dyslexia and believe in their potential, the students sense it and put forth greater efforts to succeed in the classroom. When students with dyslexia realise that their teachers care about them, their level of academic motivation improves. The degree to which a student considers his teacher as 'caring' strongly affects their motivation[6]. Caring teachers are those who demonstrate democratic interaction styles, providing constructive feedback and have good expectations for their students' behaviour. The more students with dyslexia perceive their teachers care about them, the more motivated they become. A student with dyslexia is far more responsive to a teacher who cares and is therefore more likely to learn and engage.

Connecting with your students with dyslexia establishes trust, which is important to the students' learning because it makes them comfortable enough to participate, ask for help when needed and pay closer attention to advice and encouragement. Also, students with dyslexia feel better about themselves if they feel that a teacher has taken a genuine interest in them especially with younger students who are away from their parents and overwhelmed by the classroom experience. A caring teacher is comforting and helps make the transition easier. In my view, you can pay a teacher to teach but it is hard to put a monetary value on the teachers who, in addition to teaching, actually do care.

Be inspirational

Inspiration is one of the most important gifts a teacher can provide students with dyslexia. A teacher that inspires is a role model, an influence that goes far beyond academic achievement. Most adults can recall a specific teacher from their childhood who had a lasting impact. These are the teachers that have inspired, challenged and motivated students enough to be memorable years later. Students with dyslexia who are inspired by their teachers can accomplish great things and their motivation stays with them. Inspiration takes many forms, such as: Helping students through their academic year, highlighting future aspirations and future accomplishments, enabling them to stay focused and assisting them with writing their short-term goals, time management and study skills. Many of us always cite particular teachers who taught us great lessons during our formal education or those who said great things to us when we were young that always stayed with us. We tend not to remember every single teacher who ever taught us but for some of us who are lucky, we remember one or two teachers who inspired us.

What makes teachers inspirational? Inspirational teachers represent success to their students. They make their classroom an exciting environment for learning. They hold students' fascination, engagement challenge and interest. An excellent report by the Education Development Trust in the UK (2016) differentiates between inspiring teachers and inspiring teaching[7]. Inspiring teaching is the spark that kick starts students' imagination using a 'combination of intellectual challenge, high expectations and mutual trust between teacher and learner that invites the learner to join the teacher on a journey of discovery'. Inspiring teachers are the ones who consistently strive to enhance their knowledge of the learner and their deep knowledge of the subject matter as well as consistently reflect and adjust their daily practice always asking: How can we teach this better, how can we explain this better and how can we facilitate learning more in this instance?

Great teachers are not simply born. You can become an inspiring teacher too. All you need to do is to aspire to inspire. Start first by building a strong relationship with your students with dyslexia and ensure that they know you care. Also remember that being a great inspiring teacher is not just about the knowledge you give to your students with dyslexia but about the way you encourage them, engage them and the way you lift their morale and give them sincere advice and genuine feedback.

Be grateful

'The essence of all beautiful art, all great art, is gratitude' Friedrich Nietzsche[8]. 'Gratitude unlocks the fullness of life. It turns what we have into enough, and more. It turns denial into acceptance, chaos to order, confusion to clarity. It can turn a meal into a feast, a house into a home, a stranger into a friend' Melody Beattie[9]. Gratitude is based on two major assumptions: First, our own affirmation that there is goodness in this world around us and secondly our recognition that the sources of such goodness is outside of us. One of the famous quotes of Rumi regarding gratitude is: 'The sun never tells the earth you owe me'. That is why gratitude has been thought of as the secret behind motivation. Gratitude and motivation are close and as soon as you are grateful for the things around you, it becomes easy to motivate you.

Feeling grateful enables us to reflect on our relationships with others and leads us to feel closer and more connected. This increased feeling of closeness helps motivate and sustain our efforts at self-improvement. If you are a teacher who is grateful by nature for what you have and is happy with what you are doing, invest time and effort to teach your students with dyslexia gratitude. Advise them to perhaps make a list every morning of the things they are grateful for. Train your students with dyslexia to start a gratitude diary and explain to them that they will be keeping a diary for a week in which they will record three good things that happened to them each day. They should provide an explanation of how they achieved or contributed to those good things. Encourage them to really think deeply about those positive things.

The same applies to students with dyslexia who experience the ups and downs of being dyslexic and the low self-esteem that accompanies it sometimes. To move forward and start feeling better, students with dyslexia need to experience gratitude. It is much easier for them to work through their points of weakness during that dreaded literacy intervention session when they are grateful rather than working through it while they are feeling inadequate and sorry for themselves. Advise your students with dyslexia to make a list of all the bad situations they were in and try and think of the lessons those bad situations taught them. This exercise will starve their ingratitude and feed their feeling of gratitude. This needs to be repeated many times for motivation to kick in. Help them find one tiny thing about each bad situation that ended up being a good thing. Teach them to write a 'thank you' note for someone with a sense of gratitude.

Be patient

I love quotes and I admire Oscar Wilde a lot as a writer. One of his funny quotes is: 'If you are not too long, I will wait here for you all my life'. This quote refers to patience which is a fundamental personal quality every good and inspiring teacher should possess. Patience is the ability to tolerate perceived delay. Patience is not something we literally have (although we say that sometimes); it is rather something we consciously *do*. Patience is like any other hard-earned discipline: The more we do it and practise it, the more patient we become. It is therefore vital that teachers are patient enough to listen and understand what students with dyslexia are going through. Some people find impatience a virtue and for those people, burnout is what they feel just around the corner. Impatient teachers do not take the time they need to make anything worthwhile. Often people confuse being patient with having no sense of urgency or with the inability to do things quickly. This is not the case. Being impatient in completing a task will result in the task suffering from it. It is impossible for quality and impatience to coexist. It is not possible for your student with dyslexia to be doing his current activity well when he is only thinking of being done with it or if he is in fact thinking of the next activity.

Dealing with a large classroom requires patience. It may be slightly more difficult to manage a younger group of students and in such situations exercising patience is the best way forward. Impatience leads to scattered thoughts and disorganised work so train and teach your students with dyslexia not to lose motivation to the unorganised rushing mind of impatience. Patience will enable your students with dyslexia to have their tasks planned where it is easier to focus on the current task. Your students with dyslexia will be patient when they become more realistic in their expectations. Although optimism is good, unrealistic optimism about uninterrupted smooth sailing can disturb and even sabotage the completion of important pending tasks. Patient students view setbacks as temporary. Repeat for them and train them that 'this, too, shall pass' and that patience is a real virtue that will come round and lift them. Anything worthwhile takes time to grow and mature. Train your students with dyslexia to keep the mentality of the problem-solver, not the victim. Problem-solvers look at negative situations to discover what they can do better to improve. They work consciously and continuously in keeping their own internal reactions positive and constructive.

Be enthusiastic

Teachers' enthusiasm is an important part of the learning environment. Being enthusiastic as a teacher will ensure your learners enjoy their lessons and are able to learn. Not only that, in fact enthusiasm rubs off, especially when it comes to learning new materials. The more your student with dyslexia witnesses your genuine enthusiasm about learning, the more likely they are to become enthusiastic about learning themselves. Teacher enthusiasm has an effect on student emotional engagement. Such an effect is always referred to as *emotional contagion*, whereby teachers transfer their enthusiasm and energy to students. Although emotions occur internally, they are largely shared and contagious, creating collective emotions. This is because our motivation to learn is subject to the influence of social and external contexts and one such external context is a teacher's emotion and enthusiasm.

Part of being a motivated teacher comes through your general behaviour, attitude and enthusiasm. Students with dyslexia are more attracted to teachers who regularly smile and who offer a happy and cheery outlook on life and generally those who come across as upbeat and pleasant to be with or to be around. Making your classroom a warm, colourful and stimulating environment is key to creating a positive space. Regardless of the subject you teach, help your students with dyslexia see that learning is a journey of exciting new discoveries. Take every opportunity to discover new information with them. As your students see the joy and excitement learning brings to your life, they will begin to share your enthusiasm for learning new things as well.

The more enthusiastic and dynamic teachers are, the more engaged students with dyslexia become in all aspects of school life whether it is behaviourally, cognitively or emotionally. An enthusiastic teacher creates a wonderful ambience inside the classroom with mixed feelings of excitement, enjoyment and anticipation. An enthusiastic teacher engages students with dyslexia and encourages them to participate and stimulates them to explore. A teacher's enthusiasm sparks curiosity among his students with dyslexia which in turn leads to better results in their evaluations, a more positive attitude towards their teachers, better overall school performance and most importantly enhanced and prosocial class-room behaviour. Students with dyslexia who perceive their teachers as enthusiastic, dynamic and energetic are more likely to be interested, curious, intrinsically motivated to learn and fully engaged.

Build a rapport

A rapport is a special type of a relationship or a connection you have with people that can be described as harmonious and sympathetic. Good teachers build rapport with their students with dyslexia to increase their motivation[10]. There are many tips on how to build a good rapport. First of them is for you to know your students' names and use them right from the start. You can ask about your students' hobbies, their interests, aspirations, weekend plans and acknowledge their birthdays. Showing a sense of humour and your availability for your students with dyslexia before, after and outside the classroom increases the chances of building a rapport with your students. Sharing personal insights and experiences with the rest of your class and relating your subject materials to everyday life examples and appreciating that students with dyslexia may occasionally have problems or bad days that hinder their progress are also good tips to build rapport with them. Once you know your students with dyslexia by name and know more information about their background, you can use personalised examples that are relevant to them during your lesson explanation. As a teacher, make sure to extend your students a warm and friendly invitation from the start of the school year to join the 'community of learning' that you attempt to establish in your classroom.

Rapport has a positive effect on academic achievement of students with dyslexia and on their motivation. Rapport tends to increase your students' enjoyment of the learning experience and of the subject matter. It motivates them to come to class more often, and to pay more attention. Thus, rapport seems to facilitate both the motivation of students with dyslexia for learning and their enjoyment of the course, and enhances their ability to be more receptive to what is being taught. When students with dyslexia feel that they have a good rapport with their teachers, their motivation increases, and they tend to answer more freely and with a better degree of openness. Rapport leads to satisfaction and increases understanding and comprehension. Teachers and students with dyslexia understand each other better when there is rapport between them. Although trust is necessary for rapport to develop, trust in itself can also be an outcome. Once rapport has been established, trust between teacher and student grows. No one is saying that rapport leads to learning. However, rapport certainly helps to create conditions conducive to learning. Rapport, higher motivation, increased comfort and enhanced communication all lead to better learning. Teaching does not always result in learning either, but, like rapport, it is one of those factors that can contribute positively to learning.

Develop respectful relationships

The teacher–student relationship is at the heart of teaching and students with dyslexia are not going to learn from someone they do not like. To truly inspire and motivate our students with dyslexia, you should know them well on a personal level, i.e., their interests, hobbies, friends, family situation and what excites them[11]. You should show them respect and value their individuality and you should always be kind and polite to them. While giving them feedback, be honest, accurate and offer them second chances. Depending on the personality of each student, you would realise that they would probably require different motivational strategies and knowing your students with dyslexia well can enable you to predict which strategies would work. To know your students with dyslexia on that level is to actually build and develop a meaningful and respectful relationship with them. A meaningful and respectful relationship with a student with dyslexia should be close and supportive but not overly dependent. A good teacher believes that every student in his class can learn, but differently and at different rates. A good teacher sets high expectations for their students with dyslexia, i.e., they are warm and trusting, and always endeavours to keep the relationship without conflict.

Hamre and Pianta (2001) found that for students at all ages prior to university and college levels, a positive student–teacher relationship increases engagement, motivation, prosocial behaviour and academic achievement[12]. They also reported that relationships that are based on prolonged tension and conflicts between students and teachers specially during kindergarten and early years tend to predict worse grades, work habits and discipline problems into late elementary and middle school. On the other hand, during preschool and kindergarten years and when relationships with teachers are more emotionally supportive and less conflicting in nature, it is generally noticed that preschool students become more socially and academically competent. Close and positive student–teacher relationships are always associated with greater student engagement in learning and better social and behavioural outcomes in general. During secondary school years, students with dyslexia who connect with their teachers and have good relationships built on trust, respect and appreciation are less likely to engage in risky antisocial behaviour.

Build good peer relationships

Good social skills are very important for learning, school life and for life success in general. Students' social skills include what they say to others, how they make friends and keep them and how they work well with others. It also includes how they make good choices and how they act in different social situations inside and outside their classroom. Of course, it goes without saying that how students with dyslexia function inside the classroom can impact their academic performance and their behaviour. It can also have an impact on their interpersonal relationships and participation in classroom activities as well as extracurricular activities. However, it must be noted that as students with dyslexia grow older, the influence their peers have upon them increases. That is why problems and conflicts students with dyslexia might have with their peers can make them feel less secure about their place inside the school which in turns increases their stress levels and lowers their motivation. Conflicts, peer challenges and bullying are extreme examples of bad peer relations that have a determinantal effect on students' learning. Students with dyslexia who do not have adequate social skills tend to experience anxiety and in extreme cases depression or they may display aggressive behaviour as they feel rejected by their peers.

Teachers are advised to keep an eye on the social peer relationships among their students and in particular pay special attention to their students with dyslexia. Before teachers can reflect on appropriate social skills interventions for their students with dyslexia, they have to first determine the exact skills their students need to possess so that their peer relations are enhanced. The ability to learn is built on a foundation of healthy and comfortable relationships with others including peers. Classroom learning is all about learning with and in the presence of others, and students with dyslexia who surround themselves with academically focused and goal-oriented peers, especially among high school students, will be more likely to appreciate and internalise such features themselves. Peers are important for students' social development and in particular they are important for the development of empathy, care, social responsibility, negotiation, cooperation and conflict resolution. Teachers can take a proactive approach in promoting positive peer relationships among their students with dyslexia inside the classroom by developing specific strategies in the following areas: Teaching social–emotional skills, explaining conflict resolution skills as well as problem-solving skills. Teachers are also encouraged to get their students with dyslexia to learn in groups and create a classroom climate of positive peer relationships.

Create belonging

Another important aspect of student motivation is their own feeling that they belong within the school community. Studies confirm that when students with dyslexia believe they belonged within the school community, they demonstrate higher levels of academic motivation than those students who do not feel they belong[13]. A strong positive relationship exists between students' perception that they relate or belong in their school community and their academic engagement[14]. Belonging, or having close relationships with individuals within the school or with the school social groups and taking part in school activities have all been shown to be a significant factor in school motivation. A study was performed with 580 African American, 948 Asian American, 860 Latino and 3,142 European American students (47% male and 53% female) from seven ethnically diverse high schools[15]. The students' sense of belonging, as measured by a friendship nominating activity, time spent in extracurricular activities and bonding with the teacher, contributed to student motivation and success across several different ethnic groups. In addition, it has been shown that students perform better and are more motivated in environments where they sense community and relatedness[16].

Osterman (2000) reviewed research related to the importance of students' experiencing a sense of belonging in school. According to this review, students' level of academic motivation increases when they believe they belong within the school community. Interestingly, however, students' perception that their teachers accept them is more important than their parents' or friends' acceptance[17]. It is important to note however that if a person does not feel safe within their environment or arrives to school hungry and afraid, they most likely will not feel as if they belong. When people do not have their basic need of belonging met, their motivation decreases[18].

Invite guest speakers

A professional and an experienced guest speaker can create an impact on your students with dyslexia inside the classroom if invited to address them. Making learning relevant is achieved when you invite a real-life guest speaker to address your students with dyslexia regarding their profession or their experience related to the subject matter being discussed. Guest speakers are perceived as role models that students can identify with. Policemen, firemen, local authors, entrepreneurs, nurses, medical doctors, accountants and philanthropists are various examples for guest speakers. Looking at the uniform of such guest speakers or asking them pertinent questions will not only inspire students with dyslexia but would also enable them to make up their mind and take their career decisions by asking specific questions related to their life and work. There is a good chance this will happen if you ensure that the guest speaker understands what the class is about and how what they are going to talk about is relevant to themselves and the learning experience of the students they are addressing.

Guest speakers are one excellent source for enhancing students' educational experiences because they expose students to real life experiences from the position of someone who has been there and someone who has done this before or is doing it now. Students with dyslexia get to see first-hand the insight and perspective of the guest speaker's particular field. If the guest speaker is an accomplished dyslexic or someone who suffered during his school years but managed to overcome the obstacles, students with dyslexia will find this extremely motivating. By interacting with the guest speaker and asking him questions, students with dyslexia get a real life experience and chance to connect and make a link between what they have to learn in their textbook and what the guest speaker is telling them. This is one way of externally validating this information and making it relevant for their learning purposes.

Ensure that you prepare your students with dyslexia about the topic that the guest speaker will be talking about. Run some trial sessions with them regarding what type of questions they should ask that would benefit them the most. Also make sure that after the guest speaker leaves, you debrief your students with dyslexia to double check that they benefitted and that they are happy with the answers to their questions. Inviting guest speakers also enables students to think of alternative career opportunities particularly those that do not depend heavily on perhaps written work or advanced literacy skills for students with dyslexia. Also, you might want to focus on inviting guest speakers whose skills are relevant to the dyslexics among your class to showcase to the students with dyslexia that you can be successful in your career after you finish your schooling because you are gifted now with a set of skills that would enable you to work and excel after graduation.

Have one-to-one conversations

Learning is a personal and an emotional process. Students with dyslexia always wrestle with the materials they are learning, the type of relationships inside and outside the classroom they are building and developing, and sometimes it can all get too stressful for them. To counterbalance this and to alleviate such a stress, developing stronger personal connections with their teachers is very beneficial[19]. Therefore, for you to be an effective and motivating teacher, devote some time to have one-to-one conversations with all of your students especially those with dyslexia. Do so as regularly as possible and you can organise your time to have such regular one-to-one conversations every three or four weeks. If you aim to do one a day for around 10 minutes, you will for sure get a chance to go round everyone regularly at least four or five times throughout the school years. By doing so, you will end up knowing your students as individuals and will have more insight into their learning styles, aspirations, strengths and weaknesses as well as their study skills and their time management skills.

Such meetings will change the culture inside the classroom as you will feel more connected as a teacher to your students with dyslexia and that feeling is reciprocated. You will also be better at connecting them to each other because you would know them closer and have more time talking about their interests and worries.

When a student with dyslexia has a chronic problem, pull them aside and talk to them. Ask questions and try to understand why they are struggling. Ask them what needs to change and what needs to happen for them to become successful. Work with them to develop a personal plan for them together and then help them stick to it by meeting them regularly one-to-one and ask them for updates. Find time for such meetings perhaps when students are working on their independent work after lessons or for those students who attend after-school activities, after-school lessons or after-school programmes. Sometimes they can even come and see you before the school starts early in the morning specially if you both tend to arrive earlier to school. You will notice immediate results for this idea on their overall behaviour, school grades and overall demeanour. Having those one-to-ones with your students especially those with dyslexia enables you to direct them to their colleagues or their study friends who can help them out. When you know your students as people, you can better understand what they need, and you can work more effectively to meet those needs.

Manage learners' anxiety

Anxiety is an emotional state characterised by a feeling of tension, apprehension and worry. The person experiencing anxiety feels it as tension in his muscles, irritability, fatigue, restlessness and insomnia. It leads to distorted cognitive processes such as poor concentration and unrealistic evaluation of problems and worries. It also results in poor problem-solving skills, poor coping strategies, task avoidance and procrastination. Feeling a little anxious sometimes is acceptable as we all experience feelings of anxiety sometimes. However, when it is excessive and continues for longer periods of times, it ends up being debilitating and inhibiting. Regular anxiety becomes a disorder when students have out-of-proportion responses to things most of us cope with easily. Anxiety disorders[20] are the most common of all child and adolescent mental health disorders, both in the United States and around the world. Anxiety is the most common mental health challenge that young people face, and it is the top reason why students seek mental health services at college today. In severe cases, anxiety may stop students from doing their homework, reaching out to their friends and in extreme circumstances even leaving their homes.

The Organization for Economic Cooperation & Development (OECD)[21] produced a very informative report entitled: 'How is students' motivation related to their performance and anxiety?', where they studied and analysed data from so many countries and found that students who aim higher end up going further[22]. Those students make the necessary effort to reach their goals and as they progress, they receive encouragement from their parents and teachers to aim even higher. Similarly, low levels of motivation may lead to poor performance, which could fuel further frustration and lower motivation. But there may be drawbacks to high levels of motivation. As their results show that students who are more motivated also have greater anxiety[23]. For these students, teachers may find that they are most motivated by learning that struggling with a subject is not the end of the world. Offer support no matter what the end result is and ensure that students do not feel so overwhelmed by expectations that they just give up. Motivation seems to be more closely linked to anxiety when it is imposed by others. Students who feel undue pressure to meet the expectations of their parents or teachers, or who constantly compare themselves with others, may feel tenser and more anxious.

Track learners' progress

As discussed in the 'Setting Goals' idea, before reaching a final goal, it is great to set short-term goals first. This is why it is vital to track the way studying improves. If you do this, students with dyslexia can see their progress and achievements, and if you put emphasis on improvement, it can inspire your students with dyslexia to work harder and obtain better results. Tracking progress helps students with dyslexia stay focused on what is important in order for them to reach their goal. It helps them identify potential obstacles and strategies for how to overcome them. It can also help them set more realistic goals, adjust previously set ones and stay positive along the way. Generally, when it comes to our progress, we are usually quicker to see the negative over the positive. Tracking student progress helps learners uncover such potentially harmful habits/ misconceptions regarding their own abilities and development. Teachers can use diagrams, simple charts or color-coding and literally show their students how far they have come. Just measuring their own activity can push your students with dyslexia to move more because by merely measuring their activity, they should see an improvement. Needless to say, it also helps if they establish a baseline for their tracking before it starts. Students with dyslexia who track, know immediately when they have stopped making progress or when they are off course. This allows them to course-correct and figure what went wrong and why.

One of the best ways to track their own progress is for your students with dyslexia to plan and track their actions weekly. At the beginning (or end) of each week, teach them to plan out what you want to get done. They should reference their goals for the month and make sure they are on track to achieve them. If they are not, they should simply adjust accordingly and plan to spend time where they need to during the week. Tracking gives them something to celebrate and pushes them to keep progressing towards their goal. Students with dyslexia who track their progress stay on track because they are paying attention to their own behaviour. A multi-year tracking study of the day-to-day activities, emotions and motivation was conducted to measure the levels of hundreds of knowledge workers in a wide variety of settings to uncover the top motivator of performance[24]. The study looked at: Incentives, clear goals, interpersonal support, recognition and support for making progress. Progress came out on top. When students with dyslexia feel like they are making headway and progress in their work, motivation is the highest. Once they figure out their baseline, keeping track will help them measure their improvement. Celebrating their wins, even the small ones, is a big part of keeping their confidence and motivation high.

Verbalise intentions

Motivation is what gets us to act and it springs from our intentions. Once we intend, the question follows: How are we going to be motivated to achieve our intention? Intention is *what* we want to create, and motivation is *how we feel* about it; so intention feeds motivation. Intention without motivation will not hold up and becomes more like daydreaming. However, simply wanting to do something and actually planning to do it leads to different outcomes. Students with dyslexia who plan their intention by writing down how they are going to do it end up following through. This happens because they give words to what they want and what they plan to do to achieve it. Talking about their intentions to those they trust and are close to them is a powerful way of starting the process of giving it a shape and form. Telling someone their plans helps them ensure that those intentions become a priority. It holds them accountable for taking the necessary steps to make it happen; because after all, they actually said they would. Not sharing their intentions and goals with others, it becomes easier for them to ignore and neglect. Picturing exactly what it will look like when they achieve their goal increases its potential for becoming reality. Verbalising and writing down their intentions would enable them to spend time visualising the details and feelings associated with achieving their intention. Spending their school life and performing their school work with intention means that your students do things on purpose and that they know why they are doing them.

By verbalising their intentions, your students with dyslexia are actually bringing them into their conscious reality. When they actually verbalise their intentions and hear them, not just think about them, they engage more of their brain in the activity and they will become less likely to get distracted. Reciting their intentions at the start of the day changes their mood and they are more likely to make progress. Train your students with dyslexia to differentiate between intention and motivation. Also train them to pay special attention when choosing their words. Rather than saying, 'I would like to be successful at school', they should take their time and reflect and include the details of their intention. Their word choice should reflect their true intentions so that it is easier to achieve them. At the beginning, verbalising their intentions in front of their colleagues might be slightly intimidating. However, tell them that speaking about what they want helps make it true. Also, repetition in both thought and their spoken words make all the difference. When your students with dyslexia say what they believe to be true repeatedly, it helps them become less embarrassed about it and it motivates them to achieve it.

Make learners accountable

Some students with dyslexia will sometimes make excuses and try to blame their poor grades on their teachers, fellow students, their parents or on the curriculum in general without assuming any responsibility for their actions. Students with dyslexia respond productively when teachers give them the opportunity to take charge of their academic success. By holding your students with dyslexia accountable for their work effort, you can provide them with the necessary tools they need to better themselves. This is because accountability leads to responsibility, and students who develop the tools to target and improve their academic shortcomings will, in turn, develop the skills they need to go far in life. Although making your students with dyslexia accountable for their own success and for their own learning is not easy, there are some approaches to help you help your students become responsible learners.

Greeting your students with dyslexia at the door is a good practice as it establishes confidence and a feeling of welcome into the classroom. Do not sit down a lot when students are in the classroom and move around frequently while speaking to your students. Use your eye contact and your facial expression before your words to address any inappropriate behaviour whenever possible. If you have to talk to a student with dyslexia about their behaviour, do so briefly, quietly and as a matter-of-fact. Treat your students with dyslexia as adults and remind them that they are part of a larger class. Send the message through your demeanour and tone that you care about your students, but you also hold them accountable.

Students should have the opportunity to take charge of their learning and academic success by formulating and following through on their own plan to improve. By assuming responsibility for their mistakes, students with dyslexia learn the true value of personal accountability. To ensure that students are held accountable at home and school, and to boost the likelihood that they will follow through on efforts to reach their goals, include their parents in the conversation. This will increase their positive reinforcement, which encourages them to reach their goals and also teaches them the value of personal responsibility. You can also come up with an effort and achievement rubric as a way to get your students with dyslexia to take responsibility for their learning. Create an effort and achievement scale that students complete daily or weekly to show how they are meeting their responsibilities. Students with dyslexia can grade their commitment to schoolwork periodically on a scale (from 1 to 4 for example). At the end of the month, they tally their scores on a graph and explain what the graph says about their approach to learning. Students with dyslexia also create a list of up to 10 learning targets. Each month, they give themselves a grade indicating how well they have met their objectives.

Be wise with homework

For students with dyslexia, homework can be both frustrating and upsetting[25]. More homework does not necessarily mean more learning. So teachers are encouraged to be considerate to this fact and consider homework for students with dyslexia outside of the existing rules, as it is an important part of accommodating and catering for their needs. Only valuable and necessary homework should be assigned to students with dyslexia. By limiting the quantity of the homework for students with dyslexia, teachers can really then focus on the quality of the homework itself. If your students with dyslexia have extracurricular activities after school (because many dyslexics love such activities because they excel in and enjoy them), then try not to assign homework for them during those days. Also, your students with dyslexia may forget the homework assigned to them, so it is always advisable to actually write it down in a dedicated homework journal or perhaps have a section of the website of your school (if of course you have that system in place) dedicated to recording and expanding the homework required. This will overcome the issue of your students with dyslexia forgetting what is required from them.

In some situations and if the rules allow it, increase your communication with the parents of your students with dyslexia and make sure you send them homework assignments so that they can follow up with their children at home[26]. You can do that also by dedicating a homework handout and remind your students with dyslexia to take it with them and make sure they put it inside their bags. Teachers should work with parents about big homework projects and when are they supposed to be handed in. Another way of helping your students with dyslexia and motivating them through homework is to accept proof of learning in different formats than the rest of the typically achieving students; i.e., instead of asking them to write an essay on a particular topic as their homework, can they present a project? Can they present a mind map of the essay rather than writing the essay itself? Can they type it and hand it typed instead of handwritten? All of these are tips that would really motivate students with dyslexia concerning the important issue of homework. Train your students to break down their homework into smaller manageable parts with frequent breaks between them. Train them and reach out to their parents to establish a daily homework routine too. A daily homework routine provides them with a structure that will overcome their short-term memory problems and their tendency to get lost and forget what is required of them.

Notes

1 Brophy, 1988.
2 Brewer, DeJong & Stout, 2001.
3 Hancock, 2002.
4 Stipek et al., 1995.
5 Brewer & Burgess, 2005.
6 Wentzel, 1997.
7 Inspiring Teachers; How teachers inspire learners, 2016, www.education developmenttrust.com.
8 www.goodreads.com/quotes.
9 www.passiton.com/inspirational-quotes.
10 O'Connor & McCartney, 2007.
11 Adams & Christenson, 2000.
12 Hamre & Pianta, 2001.
13 Stipek, 1996.
14 Osterman, 2000.
15 Hamm & Faircloth, 2005.
16 Stipek, 1996.
17 Osterman, 2000.
18 Maslow, 1943.
19 Burton, 2004.
20 Understanding Anxiety in Children & Teens, 2018.
21 www.oecd.org.
22 Mo, 2019.
23 Riddick et al., 1999.
24 Harkin et al., 2016.
25 Cooper & Lindsay, 2000.
26 Cooper et al., 1998.

Utilise interactive games

Students with dyslexia enjoy games and interactive activities and teachers are advised to use them as much as possible[1]. In the UK, there are specialist providers for such games and activities like Crossbow Education[2] for instance which specialises in producing games and activities on literacy, numeracy and study skills for students with dyslexia. 'Spingoes' is one such nice game that is made of a bingo spinner which allows students with dyslexia to practise their onset and rhyme. 'Funics'[3] is another game they produce which is practical in nature and is full of activities for students with dyslexia to practise rhyming words, blending, segmenting and syllable manipulation as well as phoneme identification. Other literacy games produced by Crossbow Education for students with dyslexia include: The Alphabet Lotto, the 'Bing-Bang-Bong', the 'Magic-E Spinit', the 'Hotwords' and the 'CVC Spring'. From their names, these are excellent games that enable students with dyslexia to practise their short vowel sounds and to develop their phonological awareness skills.

Teaching reading through games or 'TRUGS' for short is another brilliant card game that they produce for beginning readers. Their different styles of educational card games allow variability to suit different learners' style and are an excellent example of how you can assist students with dyslexia and motivate them by utilising those interactive literacy and numeracy games. Another provider for such literacy games and activities are Smart Kids[4] who produces a big selection of interesting and creative resources that are extremely motivating for students with dyslexia. Among their selection of games are: Smart Chute, Smart Phonics, cluster word-building games, CVC board games, alphabet practice cards, sentence builder and blend magnets. All such activities and games provide fun and utilise manipulatives which make learning multisensory for students with dyslexia. They are experiential and interactive in nature and can be very motivating for students with dyslexia.

Use look, cover, write and check strategy

The Look, Cover, Write and Check is a well-established strategy for teaching and working with spelling. In this strategy, the student first looks closely at the word which he needs to reproduce and finger traces it which enables that multisensory input of information. Two modalities or sensory channels are used during this stage, i.e., the visual through the first look followed by kinaesthetic which is the finger tracing. Both steps need to be practised and in particular paying attention to the visual shape of the actual target word[5]. During this stage, the teacher can aid by explaining the visual similarities and the words within words that one can pay attention to sometimes in order to remember words and be able to use them and spell them. The next step in this strategy is for the student to cover the target word and try to work his visual short term memory to remember the word utilising the visual image he has built and the finger tracing he exercised.

Once the above is done, the student is now ready to have a go at writing the target word himself. This is a very important stage as it involves again the visual senses along with the tactile one but while writing the word this time round and not just tracing it like before. During this stage, students with dyslexia get the chance to practise their visual and kinaesthetic memory. Once students have finished the writing stage, then comes the final feedback step which is to uncover and check how they did which provides an instant feedback that reinforces the learning content. It is important that when you are trying this activity over and over again with your students with dyslexia, they know at the beginning that it is ok to make mistakes and that mistakes are part of our learning process. Mistakes mean that they are learning so long as you encourage them to focus on the process itself and to verbalise their thoughts when visualising the word that they need to spell and focus on the visual representation of that word.

That last Check step is quite motivating for students with dyslexia especially when they come up with the correct spelling. The whole process will be strange at the beginning, but teachers are advised to persevere with it and take their time to explain the various stages of it and focus on every step until your students with dyslexia master them. Both the visual memory and the tracing elements really help your students overcome their short-term memory problems and overcome some of the peculiarities of the English spelling conventions. You can apply this strategy yourself with your spelling list or you can purchase some games and use this strategy with games to boost your students' spelling abilities.

Use the S.O.S strategy

The Simultaneous Oral Spelling strategy (S.O.S strategy for short) is a commonly used strategy that helps improve reading and spelling abilities of students with dyslexia. Due to the well documented weakness students with dyslexia have in their phonological abilities including both their poor phonemic and phonological awareness skills, this strategy is very beneficial in allowing them the chance to practise sound categorisation and rhyme through word games[6]. The S.O.S. strategy uses visual, auditory and kinaesthetic learning modalities all at the same time during spelling dictation. Younger students find the S.O.S. Strategy interesting and motivating. Although it takes a great deal of focus and concentration, once students know the steps involved, they can move through them easily. Teachers who have students with dyslexia who have weak phonological awareness or poor spelling ability are encouraged to use this strategy.

The S.O.S. strategy involves the following six steps:

1 Teacher dictates the word to the student while they are looking at the teacher to observe the way of its pronunciation and especially how the mouth moves,
2 Student repeats the word back to the teacher out loud,
3 Student sounds out the word out loud using his fingers and allocates one finger to each sound,
4 Student spells the word out loud using his fingers and allocates one finger to each one letter,
5 Student writes the word down while saying it out loud, and finally,
6 Student reads the word he has just wrote out loud.

Steps 3 and 4 are important and will let you know as a teacher which sounds and which letters exactly cause challenge and confusion to your students. By breaking words down out loud into their sounds, and later on letters, teachers know straight away if their students with dyslexia are applying the phonics and spelling strategies that they taught them or not[7]. These two steps tend to encourage students with dyslexia to self-correct and self-doubt which is an excellent exercise for their repetition and learning. It also tells teachers whether more practice is needed or not to cement learning of those sounds or letters. The S.O.S. strategy enables both teachers and students to look closely at the spelling patterns which can be a motivating strategy for students who witness progress quite quickly using this strategy.

Build word lists

The use of word lists can be a successful and motivating strategy for many students with dyslexia who have spelling difficulties. Word lists are general lists composed of words that are commonly used by students with dyslexia at certain ages. Word lists can also be in the form of specific lists that focus on students' own spelling difficulties. Word lists enable students to feel a bit more secure that they can consult a word list for the correct spelling. Obviously the more the word list is used, the more familiar the student will become with the words in the list. Some teachers tend to construct individualised word lists that are subject-specific such as one for mathematics or one for chemistry. Some teachers also recommend compiling an alphabetically arranged spelling book[8] for different subjects for each year group. Such a spelling booklet or word list can include other useful information such as definitions and explanations written by students themselves. Such a spelling booklet can also contain a table showing singular and plural endings specially the irregular ones, i.e., 'vertebra' and 'vertebrae' for instance that can be problematic for students with dyslexia.

Although word lists and spelling booklets are great reminders for students with dyslexia, it is equally important that students learn such words in context, so encourage them to perhaps add sentences to the words listed in order to facilitate meaning, usage and eventually retention[9]. Parts of the words that are problematic can be colour coded or highlighted in this booklet. Such a booklet can then be kept with the student with dyslexia most of the time and they can add to it whenever they are met with interesting and challenging words. It becomes their special booklet and they tend to have ownership of it, and they enjoy compiling and adding to it. This of course gives students with dyslexia a sense of control over, and pride in, their learning.

Encourage pre-writing activities

Writing is extremely difficult for students with dyslexia. Writing requires a great deal of focus to choose the right vocabulary and to spell them correctly. Writing also requires the identification of correct grammatical patterns and proper sentence structure techniques to convey the right meaning to the reader you are writing for. In my opinion, it is therefore the most complex task for students with dyslexia. That is why pre-writing activities are important to help facilitate the process of writing for students with dyslexia. It allows them to think more concretely about their assignment or topic. Many students with dyslexia do not succeed in their written work because there has not been sufficient pre-task preparation. Teachers are advised to encourage their students with dyslexia to plan their written work. Pre-task preparation can prevent demotivation for students with dyslexia who get overwhelmed by their written tasks and do not know where or how to start.

Examples of pre-writing activities that can assist your students with dyslexia and motivate them include: Focused free-writing, mind mapping, brainstorming, listing, outlining, question development and finally journaling. Creativity, i.e., thinking about how to approach a writing topic, is also helpful to train your students in. During the creativity stage, the most important aspect and the focus is on the flow of ideas. During focused free writing, students with dyslexia can write without much attention to the accuracy of their work or to its organisation. The most important feature during this pre-writing activity is meaning. The focus of this stage should be: Is the meaning clear? Is it coherent? Is there anything I missed? Is there anything extra that I should add? Mind mapping is also a great pre-writing activity that students with dyslexia will enjoy and benefit from. Mind mapping can be done on pen and paper or electronically as there are now many mind mapping software. It allows for the structure of ideas and for the focus to be on the topic of their writing as a whole and in particular it clarifies the relationship between the various subcomponents of the topic of their writing.

Pre-writing activities are a great way to help students develop their own clear reasoning. It also enables students to find week points in their arguments especially in the case of persuasive writing and expressive writing. Pre-writing activities also increase the whole writing efficiency by helping students plan their writing before actually executing it. It helps organise students' thoughts and process the order of those thoughts in the final written piece and as such facilitates understanding for the reader.

Use writing frames

Students with dyslexia often experience writing difficulties including spelling and sometimes handwriting difficulties. This is not surprising if we know that their writing abilities depend to a large extent on their reading skills, their working memory and executive functioning, which we know can be difficult for them. This, of course, leads them to have poor spelling, poor legibility, poor choice of vocabulary, poor idea development, lack of organisation of ideas and finally a low overall writing quality. Students with dyslexia may end up choosing words they can spell rather than those they want to use. Back tracking is common among students with dyslexia to ensure that their ideas, spelling, sentence structure and meaning is intact, which ends up disrupting their flow of thought. Luckily for teachers, there are writing frames that they can use to assist them in kick starting writing techniques and practice for their students with dyslexia. Writing frames can be developed by teachers themselves or can be purchased from various sources and are commercially available.

Writing frames are excellent ways to assist students with dyslexia who tend to run out of ideas and become demotivated when attempting expressive writing tasks. Some of those writing frames are ideal for whole classroom work while others are best used in a small group setting or even one-to-one. They are all designed, however, to model the actual writing process of real reports, essays, persuasive texts, instructions, explanations and discussions. Those writing frames can be in the form of arguments, discussion, story planners, explanation or persuasion. Regardless of the final writing work required, it is important to have some form of structure to help students with dyslexia with their writing tasks as they may be overwhelmed with their writing tasks. For senior students with dyslexia, essay writing can be quite a demotivating exercise if they do not receive any help. Some of them will know all the necessary information but may access it in a disorganised manner while attempting to write their essays. They may face challenges with the sequencing of the essay or with how to develop paragraphs and how to connect such paragraphs together to achieve cohesion within their essay. Utilising writing frames in order to provide a structure for those students can be very motivating as it will increase their self-confidence.

Utilise mind mapping tools

A 'mind map' is a visual representation of our own thinking. It is a visual thinking tool which displays our connected thoughts that tend to rotate around or stem from one single idea. In essence, it is a diagram used to visually display information. Mind mapping as a technique tends to be used to outline written documents or to organise students' thoughts and enhance their memory. Some students with dyslexia may have strengths in their creative thinking and visual learning modality and therefore mind mapping can certainly support them. That is why many students with dyslexia find mind mapping a simple but highly effective strategy to improve their learning and the organisation of their ideas and their overall writing techniques. Mind mapping is ideal in exploring ideas and presenting information in a visual manner as it uses keywords, colours and images to aid memory. Although the majority of teachers use pen and paper mind maps, there are also several mind mapping software that can make mind mapping appealing and engaging.

There are many benefits to using mind mapping such as: Planning, organising, note-taking, studying and writing. Mind mapping makes it easy to organise tasks and ideas in one visual display and by drawing a mind map, students' main ideas provide a starting point from which they can expand on. Mind mapping also helps break down complex information since it is an easy way to brainstorm thoughts organically without worrying about order and structure. It allows students to visually structure their ideas and therefore helps them with the analysis and recall processes. Teachers are advised to explain mind mapping techniques to their students with dyslexia and explain their benefits and advantages. Allow your students with dyslexia ample practise time to do a few different ones in a few subjects to share with you. Advise them not to worry about what their mind maps look like. After all, it is only for them to see and create and it will allow them the chance to structure their ideas. Mind maps do not have to make sense to other people as long as they make sense to your students with dyslexia and as long as they help your students with their writing and their organisation of ideas.

Some teachers may allow their students with dyslexia at the beginning only to submit mind maps as proof of learning and slowly train them on how then to develop pieces of writing from those mind maps. Students with dyslexia suffer with doing so many tasks at the same time and as such mind maps can decrease this burden by focusing on the main idea first then the order and rationale and relationships. Once these are explained and secured, students with dyslexia can then be trained to transform this into a final piece of writing while focusing on word choice, grammar, style and meaning.

Use a paired reading strategy

Paired reading is a well-known strategy to assist students with dyslexia and is also sometimes referred to as partner reading. In a typical paired reading scenario, a student reads a text with another student in order to develop his reading skills. Both students may have the same reading ability or one of them may be a better reader than the other. Although paired reading is generally known to be between two students, some people use paired reading between students and teachers or between students and their parents. At school, students with dyslexia may be paired with their teacher or with a senior student or a classmate. A paired-reading strategy is very motivating and useful for students with dyslexia because it allows for an instant visual and auditory feedback. It is a simple yet effective technique for helping students with dyslexia increase their reading speed and reading accuracy[10].

Paired reading with the teacher is generally done if there is a need to focus on one student only at a time like in a one-to-one session for instance. Teachers can read together a few times with the student until they become confident that the student can read on their own. Paired reading with a senior student in the school is generally done with the same aim as paired reading with the teacher but has an added advantage of allowing the teacher to focus on other students inside the classroom as well as bonding between different students. Paired reading with a parent is generally done at home in cases of preparation for a homework assignment or to practise reading at home. Finally, paired reading with a classmate is the most straightforward and famous one and is very beneficial for both students taking part. It is fun and rewarding for both and the feedback is instantaneous[11]. While some teachers tend to pair students of the same reading abilities, others pair more fluent readers with less fluent ones.

The paired reading strategy can be used with many types of reading materials. The strategy is useful because it frees up teachers' time to observe paired reading sessions and work with different students while their other students continue reading together and working at the same time. It is a great strategy that can be used to build oral skills so that poor or shy readers are encouraged to take part and participate in a fun reading activity. Teachers are advised to adjust the choice of partners as they see necessary, while paying special attention to the needs and feedback of their students with dyslexia[12]. To obtain the best results, teachers are advised to invest their time and efforts in establishing a routine for their students so that they know the step-by-step requirements for engaging in their paired reading activity. Teachers can ask their students to begin reading in pairs and then guide them by adjusting their reading speed.

Use pomodoro technique

The Pomodoro Technique was first invented by Francesco Cirillo during the late 1980s in which he used kitchen timers that were shaped like tomatoes; hence the word 'Pomodoro' which means tomatoes in Italian[13]. Cirillo found that by using those timers, he could in fact study for longer periods of time and focus more if these are done in short periods that are interrupted by short breaks. So the Pomodoro Technique is a time management method which traditionally uses a 25-minute block of working time before the next short break is due. Each interval is known as a Pomodoro, after the tomato-shaped kitchen timer that Cirillo used. Teachers can train their students with dyslexia on how to use this technique at home or at school. Once students decide on a task, they can then use their timers (either similar timers can be used or a smart phone) and set it to 25 minutes and start working on the task at hand. Once the time is up, students should stop working and put a checkmark on a piece of paper. If students have fewer than four checkmarks, they can take a 3- to 5-minute break, then repeat the process again. After four Pomodoros, students can take a longer break perhaps a 15- to 30-minute break. They can draw a line through the four checkmarks and start counting their checkmarks again. There are also phone applications that can do this for users now. Dozens of phone applications and even websites provide those timers as well as instructions on how to use them.

This technique has the potential to reduce the impact of both internal and external interruptions and distractions. It works because a Pomodoro cannot be further divided into smaller parts and therefore in the case of an interruption during a Pomodoro, either the interrupting activity must be postponed, or the Pomodoro abandoned and not counted. If students finish their task and they still have time left in a given Pomodoro, they can engage in various activities such as reviewing and editing the work they just completed or prepare for the coming task. If a Pomodoro begins, it has to end. Students can take advantage of overlearning by using the remaining period in the Pomodoro to review work completed or to make small improvements. There are now many variations to the Pomodoro Technique which allow teachers to tailor the principles to better suit learning and their students.

Use audio books

Naturally, students' writing skills tend to depend to some extent on their reading skills which in turn tend to depend on their listening skills. That is why it is extremely useful for some students with dyslexia who do not enjoy reading at the moment or those who find reading challenging, to listen to audio books instead[14]. Audio books help students with dyslexia become better readers and learners as they support their comprehension and boost their confidence. For students with dyslexia, being able to listen to text makes it possible for them to access as much text as they possibly can because the books they listen to are narrated by real people and most important novels and famous books are now available on audio books. Listening to text has become widespread now for students with dyslexia as well as typically achieving students. Audio books have levelled the playing field for students with dyslexia so that they too have the same opportunities now as their peers who can read easily.

Audio books allow students with dyslexia to have a positive relationship with storytelling in general and notably in the case of listening to plays or novels. By using audio books, students with dyslexia enjoy listening and gathering all of the information required of them without the frustration associated with them not being able to access the written word. Using audio books allows students with dyslexia to listen to books of interest which encourages them to engage with the text and find pleasure in reading by their ears. Although some view that listening to audio books does not have the same benefits as reading them, others do not agree and think that just because the book is audio does not mean it is less effective. The latter quote the simple view of reading which highlights the importance of oral language for reading development and argue that both (reading through the visual and auditory domains) are important for the purposes of language processing[15].

If teachers find that for some of their students with dyslexia reading is not their favourite thing to do at the moment, their next best tactic is to subject them to as many words as possible audibly. Audio books will expose those students to complex words and storylines that they would otherwise miss. For those students, audio books can open up great opportunities for accumulating knowledge. Such an exposure will promote the development of new vocabulary. Access to world knowledge and vocabulary are critical to learning and both can be facilitated by audio books, so use them.

Use assistive technology

Assistive technology is a familiar term used by teachers to provide help and support for students with dyslexia[16]. It refers to the tools or the devices that are specifically designed to help students with dyslexia learn and perform better and encourage them to become more independent. Assistive technology helps students with dyslexia save time and overcome their many challenges such as slow note-taking abilities, poor spelling, poor handwriting, disorganisation of ideas and lack of structure. This allows them to demonstrate their abilities in different ways. Assistive technology can be very helpful for students with dyslexia because it enables them to access the printed materials and present and manipulate the information that they know to consolidate their learning.

There are so many examples of assistive technology applications and programmes for students with dyslexia. These assistive technology applications and programmes can be divided according to various criteria. In terms of deficits or areas of improvements, there are assistive technology programmes for students with dyslexia that target: Reading, spelling, writing, maths, organisation of ideas, note taking and time management. Since students with dyslexia suffer from spelling for instance, there are many applications that can enable spell checkers to be installed or used by them to assist them. Also, due to their lack of structure and poor organisational skills, notably when attempting a piece of writing, students with dyslexia at various ages would greatly enjoy using mind mapping tools and programmes. Also, capturing the actual lesson by recording it is another useful tool that students with dyslexia can now enjoy using the many various devices and programmes that are making recording lessons easier than before. Changing the format between text and speech in both directions is useful for students with dyslexia who can utilise software to read the text out loud for them, or use software that can write down what they are saying.

Assistive technology is a great asset for effective teachers seeking help for students with dyslexia. Assistive technology will not, however, replace effective structured multisensory cumulative literacy instruction in reading, spelling and writing, which students with dyslexia need. Assistive technology is fun to use and comes in different shapes and colours, and enables students with dyslexia many instances of repetition and over learning and that is why teachers are advised to utilise it to motivate their students with dyslexia inside and outside of the classroom.

Promote reading at home

Promoting reading at home and discussing reading materials with students with dyslexia encourages and supports their love of learning, which in turn increases their motivation[17]. Therefore, if you would like to be an effective teacher and support and motivate your students with dyslexia, reach out to their parents and ask them to support you by encouraging their children to read at home. Advise parents about the many strategies they can utilise at home to encourage reading for their children and encourage the students themselves to do that at home. If parents of students with dyslexia read themselves, their children will see them reading and they will imitate them. Parents can make sure that their children try and read every day. Reading is a skill that needs practice and gets better with frequent practice[18]. As a teacher, try and give books as gifts or prizes and encourage parents to do so too. Advise parents not to stop reading to their children[19]. Parents can also make reading a privilege. For example, parents can read for their children or read with their children if they have done something good so reading here is a reward and a privilege.

Advise parents to make reading part of their daily life, and their children will grow to love it. Parents can take their children with dyslexia to the library to borrow books and be among books to slowly encourage a love of reading and remove the fear associated with libraries, books and reading. Parents should be advised to make reading activities with their children fun. If their child finishes reading a book that has been made into a film, parents can make popcorn and watch the movie together with their child with dyslexia and talk about the differences between the movie and the book. Advise parents to make reading a regular enjoyable part of their family routine. Some parents are not good readers themselves, but they can still encourage their children by asking their children to read to them. Parents can also devote dinner time to talk about books. Oral language and building vocabulary are very important for students with dyslexia and these can be encouraged by talking about books they read. A big vocabulary inventory is not born; it is made. Parents can help their children build this at home by encouraging their children to read at home and by talking about the books that they have read. Encourage children to use descriptive language and ask them to clarify the subtle differences in meaning between closely related words. Parents can also help promote reading at home by making reading personal and connecting the books their children read to actual real-life stories. Parents can also encourage their children to read a book series or a novel series.

Promote parental involvement

Parents and family members have an important role in supporting their children with dyslexia at school[20]. There is a positive connection between parental involvement and student achievement and when schools and teachers work to involve parents, they can increase student achievement and motivation. Parental involvement generally refers to parents' and family members' use and investment of resources in their children's schooling. Such investments can take place inside or outside of the school with the aim of improving their children's learning[21]. Parental involvement at home can include discussions about school or helping with homework assignments. At school, parental involvement may include volunteering in the classroom, attending school plays or sports day. Parental habits affect the motivation of their children such as: Showing an interest in their children's learning material, following up with them about how their day went, actively listening and taking an interest when their children discuss what happened at school, helping with homework assignments or attending parent meetings. Parental involvement is based on parents' beliefs about their roles and responsibilities and their sense that they can help their children succeed in school. When parents get involved, children's schooling is affected through their knowledge and skills as well as their increased sense of confidence that they can succeed in supporting their children with dyslexia at school.

Teachers are advised to seek the involvement of parents in the educational process of their students with dyslexia. After all, parents are your allies and your partners in the learning process, so utilise them. Build a good relationship with them and communicate with them at all times. Actively seek their help and involvement so that your efforts are both complimenting each other and the benefit will then be doubled for your students with dyslexia. Research on the effects of parental involvement has shown a consistent, positive relationship between parents' engagement in their children's education and student outcomes[22]. Parental involvement affects students' achievement because they affect students' motivation and their sense of competence and their belief that they have control over their success while at school. Teachers are therefore encouraged to create overlap between school, community and home activities so that teachers can help improve their Use mnemonic strategies

A mnemonic is an instructional strategy that effective teachers use to help their students with dyslexia improve their memory of important information. Mnemonics are extremely useful memory aides used to help students with dyslexia remember information that they need to know. The strategy enables students to connect new learning with prior knowledge through the use of cues that are witty and sometimes funny. Different types of mnemonic strategies may rely on the use of key words, rhyming words or acronyms. Teachers are advised to develop mnemonic strategies for their students with dyslexia at the beginning, but eventually they should encourage their students to come up with their own. Mnemonics are strategies that can be modified to fit a variety of learning content as they enhance memory of complex words or ideas and promote better retention of learned material. It is especially beneficial for students with dyslexia who tend to experience difficulty with information recall. Mnemonic strategies are powerful tools that increase the volume of information students remember and as such a great help for students with dyslexia to aid their information recall and spelling.

Memory for factual information is fundamental for success in school and since mnemonic strategies are systematic procedures for enhancing memory, they are very valuable in developing better ways to take in information so that it will be easier to remember. The way we encode information when we first study facilitates better memory. Teachers are therefore advised to find a way to relate new information to information students already have in their long-term memory when they consider helping them develop mnemonic strategies. Teachers should realise that initial development of many of these strategies can be difficult for their students and as such they should try developing several strategies themselves before teaching their students with dyslexia. If teachers experience difficulties themselves, the task will be much more difficult for their students. Each year, teachers can develop few strategies to accompany the content areas that they teach frequently. Over time, they will have a great number of effective strategies that they can teach their students. There are many websites, books and worksheets for mnemonic strategies that teachers can seek to assist their students with dyslexia. Some of them are really fun to use and will be greatly appreciated by students.

Encourage learners to type

Because handwriting is particularly difficult for students with dyslexia, typing generally or touch typing in particular can support them. Typing gives students with dyslexia access to the technology that can assist them by providing autocorrect, spelling checkers, grammar checkers and text-to-speech support. Typing is a much faster and more efficient and simpler way of completing the work of students with dyslexia than handwriting. Typing helps them improve their spelling, memory, vocabulary and reading skills. It also makes the writing process less frustrating and makes composing written work more fluid and effective. Also while typing, there is no distraction caused by forming letters and the presentation of work is neater without erasing marks or messy crossing out. The more students with dyslexia improve their typing skills, the more they develop automaticity so that they can type common words without thinking. This muscle memory is greatly enhanced by typing because it transforms spelling into more than patterns on the keyboard and makes mistakes in changing letter positions and sequence less common.

Some courses that teach students with dyslexia to type or touch type utilise a multisensory approach and reinforce the phonics skills of those students. Teachers are advised to let their students learning to type to train using real words instead of nonsense words. Have your students train on using similar sounding words together to reinforce their spelling patterns. But also advise them not to be overloaded by trying to learn too many skills at once. The three sub skills of typing are: (1) Knowing the keyboard layout, (2) typing accurately and (3) quickly. Therefore, interactive but short lessons can keep students with dyslexia interested as some of them find it difficult to concentrate for longer periods of time. If training sessions are interactive and fun, they are likely to attract the students to learn faster. In the past, parents of students with dyslexia would invest in buying a typing programme to improve the typing skills of their children.

However, there is now a move towards the use of online typing tutors. Many of those online typing tutors are free to use so utilise them for your students with dyslexia.

Typing for students with dyslexia offers them an easy way of correction while maintaining their presentation skills and their spelling and grammar. It also enables students with dyslexia the chance and the freedom to experiment with different styles of writing and as such develop stronger writing skills. They can always go back and correct and overwrite what they have written and focus on their choice of words, vocabulary and thoughts. For students with dyslexia who also have dyspraxia, or dysgraphia, typing is an effective way to help boost their writing skills. Instead of always having messy and illegible writing, their typed work can look good and easier to read which increases their motivation and pride in their work.

Use a structured procrastination technique

Procrastination is derived from Latin and has two components: *Pro* which means forward and *Crastinus* which means tomorrow. Those who procrastinate always put off what they ought or should do today until tomorrow because they feel that it should start tomorrow, or tomorrow is a new day or is a new start. The term 'structured procrastination' however, was first used by a Stanford University professor named John Perry who wrote an essay on the subject[23]. He explained that individuals who tend to procrastinate like to do the easy or simple tasks first and put off harder and bigger tasks to perform later. Most procrastinators will give in to the present bias which affects their priorities. As a result, the value of their short-term action or activity irrationally outweighs their long-term goal. However, he argues that the procrastinator can be in fact motivated to do the difficult tasks that are critical and important if such tasks themselves become less important or less tedious than other tasks. For this technique to work, students with dyslexia will have to think of tasks that are more important or more difficult than studying and put those tasks at the top of their to do list. Once this is done, the current original task becomes less overwhelming and less difficult to handle.

Structured procrastination means shaping the structure of the tasks your students have to do in a way that exploits their procrastination. The list of tasks they have in mind can be reordered according to their importance. The tasks that seem most urgent and important will be at the top. Worthwhile tasks to perform will be lower down on that list. Doing the less important tasks becomes a way of not doing the tasks higher up on the list. With this sort of appropriate task structure, the procrastinator becomes motivated. Structured procrastination is a re-programming of how your students procrastinate. Instead of doing meaningless marginal tasks, they do meaningful marginal tasks.

Structured procrastination works with the procrastinator because the type of procrastination that makes students with dyslexia less productive will in fact turn their weakness into a strength and motivates them to work and become more productive. Procrastinators do not avoid work or refuse work out right; they just would rather work on fun and exciting projects. So, make the assignment fun and exciting and introduce other harder and more boring assignments for procrastinators to entice them to change their set of priorities. Encourage your students with dyslexia to rank their assignments and study reviews that seem quite significant but have flexible deadlines at the top of their list. They will probably find that there are newer very important tasks that are added to their list, making that original assignment look all the more appealing.

Allow alternatives to hand-written responses

Written assessments are divided into either selected or constructed responses. A selected response is choosing the correct response from a multiple-choice task; a matching activity or a true–false activity. Multiple-choice tasks are widely used for gathering information about knowledge of facts or the ability to perform certain operations. They are easier for students with dyslexia because no written responses are required, and they are efficient because students with dyslexia answer many questions in a small amount of time. Optical mark sensors are now widely available and as such responses can be scored quickly. The other two types of written assessment involve constructed responses that may require short or long written answers or essays. Teachers of students with dyslexia are advised to allow alternative forms of hand-written responses.

Writing is a very complex task for students with dyslexia who can be motivated if allowed to submit their responses in different formats[24]. They can be allowed to submit their responses using a word processer or an iPad. They can submit their responses in the form of charts, diagrams and pictures. Performance tasks are also a great help for students with dyslexia as these are hands-on activities that require students to demonstrate their ability to perform certain actions and they also cover a wide range of activities such as designing products or experiments, gathering information, putting information in tables, analysing data, interpreting results or preparing presentations.

Senior projects or end of year projects are excellent alternatives to hand-written assessments that can be considered for students with dyslexia as they are long term and cumulative. Such assessments do not have to be written or the writing component can be carried out by someone in the group who is not dyslexic. The student with dyslexia can perform the work which does not require writing such as collecting information, analysing data or giving a presentation. Allowing students with dyslexia to also submit a portfolio to prove their learning or document their efforts is yet another great alternative to written responses.

Encourage multisensory learning techniques

Traditionally, most students with dyslexia spend most of their time inside traditional classrooms where they depend on their ears to hear the teachers and on their eyes to see them; so the predominant underlying cognitive processing that it taking place is visual and auditory processing of information. Multisensory learning provides more ways for receiving and manipulating and eventually understanding new information. If multisensory learning techniques are utilised, there will be more ways to remember information and more ways to recall it later. Because students with dyslexia typically have difficulty absorbing new information, multisensory teaching and learning techniques help break down such barriers to learning by making the abstract more concrete and by turning lists or sequences into movements, sights and sounds. Multisensory learning techniques are more fun and work well for most students so teachers are advised to adopt them.

Instead of only depending on auditory and visual information input, multisensory learning techniques also involve movement and touch. If a teacher of Mathematics uses a pizza or an orange to explain fractions and demonstrate concepts such as a whole, a half or a quarter, this learning experience will also include touch, smell and movement in addition to visual and auditory input to their students. By involving more senses and by making lessons come alive by incorporating touch, smell and taste into their lessons, teachers can help students with dyslexia learn and retain information faster and better[25]. There are many different techniques to encourage multisensory learning such as starting the lesson with a picture or an object and asking your students to illustrate it or tell a story about it and then ask them to make those stories come to life by creating a puppet show or acting the stories out. You can use different colour papers in your worksheets and encourage discussions among your students after breaking them down into smaller groups. Teachers are also encouraged to use various media for their lessons such as PowerPoints, videos, movies, pictures and worksheets. Teachers can also use games to increase the fun element in the lesson. The key in all such techniques is the use of two or more senses at the same time. Saying the word outload while tracing it is a multisensory technique. Getting young learners to trace various letters using a sand tray is also a multisensory learning technique. Using as many techniques as you possibly can will motivate your students with dyslexia.

Utilise sight word reading techniques

Sight words are words that students with dyslexia are expected to recognise instantly and become familiar with as they no longer need to decode them. Although some sight words are regularly spelled, others are spelled irregularly. Sight words are different from high frequency words. Sight words are words that students recognise immediately and can read without having to decode them while high frequency words are those commonly found in the English language. Sight words build speed while reading, which in turn increases the chances of accurate reading comprehension[26]. Sight words are common and foundational words that students with dyslexia can utilise to build their vocabulary.

Students with dyslexia feel excited when they begin to recognise words they have learned in the books they are reading. Teachers are therefore advised to keep a collection of sight word readers. These books should be made available for students to look at and read after finishing their work or to take them home with them. There are many techniques and strategies for teaching sight words. During the See & Say strategy, students are encouraged to see the sight word on flash cards prepared by teachers and then say the word while underlining it with their fingers. In the Spell Reading strategy, students are encouraged to say the word and spell the letters out before finally reading the word again. In the Arm Tapping strategy, students are encouraged to say the word and then spell the letters out while tapping them on their arm and reading the word again. During the Air Writing strategy, students are encouraged to say the word first before writing the letters in the air in front of the flash card. Finally, during the Table Writing strategy, students write the letters on a table while they are first looking at the flash cards and then are asked to write the letters again without looking at the flash cards. Moreover, teaching sight words through songs, games and by using manipulatives makes learning fun and easy. Some teachers create a Go Fish game using the words they want students to practise learning. Word Searches are another excellent game if sight words are used. 'Wordo' is a game similar to Bingo that can also be used with sight words.

Using different types of manipulatives during classroom work makes learning seem more like a game for students with dyslexia. Use large magnetic letters to build words in the case of young learners. Stamp the words using alphabet rubber stamps. Use alphabet cookie cutters or play dough letter stamps to stamp the words into play dough. Students love them because they can see them, hear them and above all touch them. Also singing a distinctive catchy tune helps your students with dyslexia remember sight words. Teachers should always check with their school libraries regarding sight word readers and if none are found, they should request them because they are a great aid for students with dyslexia.

Utilise working memory enhancement techniques

Students with dyslexia often report problems with their working memory which creates a challenge for them and makes their learning difficult. Working memory refers to holding the information briefly in the short-term memory while manipulating it. A good example of working memory is if someone is on the phone and is being given a number or an address that they have to memorise because they have no means of writing it down. Some of us would simply repeat the information over and over again either in our minds or actually verbalising it to retain it. Others would perhaps break it down to something smaller to enable us to remember it. In both cases, we depend on our working memory during learning activities. Working memory can be auditory or visual. Students with dyslexia have deficits in their working memory which makes it difficult for them to retain the image of letters and match them with sounds or to pronounce the word out loud.

There are many activities teachers of students with dyslexia can use to motivate them in order to overcome their working memory deficits such as riddles, board games or retelling stories they just listened to. Teachers can enhance poor working memory by utilising various techniques and games both inside and outside their classroom. A classic game that can be used inside the classroom to boost working memory is: 'I went to the shop and bought …'. Teachers can start the sentence and each student can add their own new item to the list. Items can be added per category (fruits for instance) or in alphabetical order if teachers wanted to make the game more challenging.

The same game can be played with a different sentence such as: 'I went on holiday and in my suitcase I packed …'. Students can be asked to simply list an object that no other student used before them or list an object and the next student repeats the previous objects and then adds their own. The more the game goes round the more difficult of course it would become because students have to remember all of the listed items and in the order they were mentioned. There are of course several variations to this game which may include sentences like: 'I went to the zoo and I saw …', or 'I went to the park and played on …'. Another game is when a variety of items are placed on a tray and the student can look at them for few seconds before the tray is covered up and they have to say how many they actually remember. Teachers are advised to ensure that their students know the names of the items before starting. Spot the difference is another great game to help with this skill as students with dyslexia will have to remember the image as they look between the two to know the difference.

Avoid copying from the board

During classroom learning, teachers generally tend to ask their students to copy information from either a notebook, a textbook or from the board. Copying from a board is challenging for students with dyslexia[27]. Some students with dyslexia may find it difficult to reproduce words accurately and have trouble finding their place on the board after they have looked down at their notebook specially when they are under pressure to do so quickly. Students with dyslexia may also have difficulties reading from a shiny white board that is causing glare and visual stress for them. Typically, copying from the board requires students to look up at the board, read a few words, hold them in their short-term memory before finally writing them down in their notebooks. Although initially they may be able to follow the task, they may get tired later and end up losing their place and making mistakes. They may confuse words, misspell them or omit words. Such a process involves a series of sequential visual and cognitive processes which is challenging for students with dyslexia.

Teachers of students with dyslexia are therefore advised to limit the amount of copying from the board their students with dyslexia are required to do. Instead, they can give their students with dyslexia copies of the notes or of the examples used in their instructions or they can use different coloured markers for their board work so as to make the content easier to understand and follow. Teachers can also slow down while giving their instructions and allow enough time for their students with dyslexia to understand the information and digest the content. Instead of predominantly depending on copying information from the board, teachers can encourage their students with dyslexia to use hands-on activities and discussions.

The offer of a note-taker, using a computer or utilising someone else's copy of the notes from the board would also help students with dyslexia a great deal. Another great tip to overcome such an issue is to train your students on note-taking strategies. Teachers should ensure that their students with dyslexia can see the board clearly and easily. Since students with dyslexia have different writing speeds, teachers are encouraged to leave the writing on the board long enough so that most students can access it and finish copying the work. It is also a good practice for teachers to put their homework tasks on the board early in the lesson and not at the end. That way, their students with dyslexia will have enough time. Some teachers also number their lines when they write using the board so that their students can find their place. Other teachers need to make sure that their writing is well spaced and clear for their students to read.

Apply differential marking principles

Students with dyslexia tend to make more spelling and grammatical errors, omit or repeat words and sometimes do not use punctuation in a correct way in their written work. They may experience other challenges in their slow reading and writing speeds which means they are often unable to produce written work as quickly as their other typically achieving counterparts. There are common signs that may be evident in the written work of students with dyslexia such as their frequent spelling errors, their punctuation, poor grammar, weak sentence structure, unreliable proofreading skills and their unsophisticated language structure. For all such reasons, it is always advisable and indeed considered part of a reasonable adjustment repertoire, to employ differential marking principles when marking the work of students with dyslexia. This is done to level the playing field for them so that they are being treated fairly and being extended equal opportunities of success and access to the curriculum similar to their typically achieving counterparts.

Teachers of students with dyslexia are advised to pay special attention when marking their written work. If they are marking for content, then they should consider carefully what students are being marked for, i.e., their factual knowledge or underlying cognitive logical ability, or their ability to produce original thought? In those three examples, spelling and punctuation might be irrelevant and teachers may elect to look beyond the actual text itself and ensure that they do not unwittingly mark a candidate down for lack of skills that are either not the focus of the current assessment at hand or irrelevant to it. However, if spelling and grammar are an important and an integral part of the actual work being measured, teachers should alert the students in advance so they are aware and devote enough time to check and proofread their own work before final submission is expected. If poor spelling does not affect the knowledge being demonstrated, students with dyslexia should not then be subjected to penalties. The same principles may also apply in the case of sentence structure, grammar and punctuation errors that do not affect the overall meaning or skill being measured. Teachers should be very clear about their marking criteria, especially the items related to spelling, grammar and punctuation. Teachers should also avoid using red markers to highlight errors because these tend to have negative associations that their students may have encountered in the past. Teachers are also encouraged to utilise error analysis while marking which tends to encourage their students to find and correct their errors for the future work.

Utilise graphic organisers to aid writing

Writing as a task is difficult for students with dyslexia and does not come easy for them and teachers should make conscious efforts to facilitate their students' writing assignments[28]. An important way of assisting students with dyslexia with their writing is the introduction of graphic organisers. A graphic organiser is a visual aid or a visual planner that shows the actual parts of writing that are required, such as a paragraph or the whole essay. A graphic organiser is helpful because it visually represents the important information required only, while eliminating the less important information. Graphic organisers are frequently utilised to assist students in organising and sequencing their thoughts. They aid in clarifying the various relationships that exist inside the written assignments students are working on. Graphic organisers may have simple lines, or circles and boxes to create images to assist students with dyslexia in organising their writing. Graphic organisers can focus on simplifying different types of relationships such as hierarchical, cause and effect or compare and contrast. Visual spacing and the graphic nature of those organisers enable students with dyslexia to organise and formulate their idea easily. Furthermore, new knowledge, concepts, thoughts and ideas inside the written work can all be explained and highlighted by using a graphic organiser.

A graphic organiser works for students with dyslexia as a strategy because they boost the working memory of students with dyslexia. Since the main classification of the ideas inside the required written assignment is already done for them by the graphic organiser, students focus more on the ideas and the sentence structures, spellings and punctuation. In addition, graphic organisers assist students with dyslexia in self-checking their work since the structure is already provided by the organiser. Teachers of students with dyslexia are therefore advised to use them and to train their students on how to use them. There are many types, and some are already free and available online to download. Some of the graphic organisers are nicely designed and attractive for students with dyslexia to use. Different types of graphic organisers tend to focus on different stages of the writing process such as brainstorming of ideas or writing the final draft of the homework assignment. Students with dyslexia can be encouraged to perform more in-depth writing assignments, which can be facilitated by using graphic organisers.

Develop learners' organisational skills

In additions to the well-established problems students with dyslexia experience in reading, writing and spelling, they also tend to have poor organisational skills that are manifested in their disorganised timetable, study, school, playtime and their disorganised school bags, personal belongings, learning materials and learning supplies. Students with dyslexia put so much energy into learning to read and write that they sometimes miss some of the organisational skills they need to be effective learners. Luckily, there are some ideas that teachers can do to assist their students with dyslexia with their organisational skills. Teachers can print class assignments and homework activities for different subjects on different coloured papers to increase organisation and enhance memory. Teachers can also include check boxes at the end of each step of their instructions so that their students can check that they have completed each step as they proceed. Students with dyslexia should be encouraged to use journals and daily planners because they are very useful tools for organising work and study. Teachers can assist by developing homework assignment worksheets that require the signatures of their students' and their parents. This will enlist the help of parents in ensuring that the work is completed and that parents are helping at home with organisational difficulties. Teachers can also work with students and their parents to develop a daily study routine.

Teachers should allocate a good amount of time and effort to explicitly teaching organisational skills and strategies to their students. Teachers can also teach various ways in which their students can prioritise their goals and aims. Students with dyslexia should also be taught to designate a specific place for their study materials so that they do not lose them often or spend unnecessary time every day looking for them. Pens, papers, laptop and notebooks should be grouped together in one place where they can be easily found. Teachers are role models and they can model organisational skills to their students with dyslexia and take time to actually talk about the importance of being organised. Teachers should also provide practical strategies to help their students overcome their organisational problems such as preparing their school bag the night before instead of doing it in the morning while waiting for the school bus to arrive.

Develop learners' time management skills

Students with dyslexia take longer and may have to work harder than their typically achieving students to accomplish reading and writing tasks and, therefore, it is very important that they know how to manage their time. That is why it is advisable to teach them how to use a timer to stay on track with the amount of time they spend on a particular task. Alternatively, they can use reminders to either stop what they are doing or to get ready to work on another task. Dedicating a small time each day or each week is also advisable for them to figure out what exactly they need accomplished. Once they know the exact tasks they need done, they can then proceed to use planners or to-do lists and plan how they are going to do them and how much time each task should take. Two important tips can also assist students with dyslexia when they are developing their time management skills: First to learn to say no to interruptions and to distractions, and secondly to actually treat themselves once they successfully complete a task in the time allocated.

We all have different times during the day when we are most likely alert and focused. Students with dyslexia need to be trained on how to observe this time in themselves and identify it. Once identified, they then need to be advised to use this particular time to tackle the tasks that are most challenging or that need the most focus. Other less focused time can then be utilised for less cognitively demanding activities. If students with dyslexia use file papers for their studies that have holes in them, they can then actually save those papers as their study notes because they would be easier to save. This will save them time copying their notes again and will keep the materials in a dedicated folder ready for them to revert back to whenever they want. Also, while studying and writing their notes, students with dyslexia can write in short-hand instead of complete sentences because this will save them time. For students with dyslexia, talking to someone about their ideas can help them clarify them and save time in the actual work or application of their idea, rather than taking time in trial and error and preparation. Keeping a diary or a journal where students can write down their ideas and draw their concept maps is another great tip to save time and manage time for students with dyslexia, especially if they have access to it at all times, while on the bus to and from school for instance. Monthly calendars are also excellent tools to manage time. Train your students to add important events to their calendar such as the holidays, music lessons or their sports practice. Once they also receive school assignments, they should add them in too.

Develop learners' study skills

One of the areas where teachers can assist their students with dyslexia and motivate them to learn is study skills. Study skills are the skills your students need to enable them to study and learn efficiently[29]. Study skills are not related to only a specific subject, but are generic and can be utilised when studying any area. Teachers of students with dyslexia are advised to train their students on how to develop their own study skills. This will increase their awareness and metacognitive abilities and make them think how they are studying and what they need to do to retain information longer and to benefit more from their subjects. Study skills involve two main aspects: Actually getting the students organised enough to start studying and then finding the time to study[30]. Getting organised is an important first step to effective study which includes where and when to study and who can assist them to study. Finding the time to study focuses on basic principles of managing their time while they are studying.

Learning styles are important prerequisites for study skills. If your students are predominantly visual learners, utilise colours, graphic organisers and mind maps. If they are predominantly auditory, they can record their notes, use text to speech software or discuss their learning with someone.

If they are kinaesthetic learners, they can handwrite or type their notes or perhaps even do a role play or an act. Moreover, know which time of day your students are most alert and what type of lights, sound and room layout really assist your students with dyslexia in their studies. Spend time with your students with dyslexia talking about study skills and make available to them a learning styles questionnaire so that they know their preferred learning style and utilise it to study. Advise your students to use different coloured folders for each subject and sticky notes to summarise their learning. Train them to make a list of all the things that distract them from their studies and how to prevent those distractors. Train them to divide their work into smaller chunks or perhaps 10 or 15 minutes each. Once you train your students on how to identify distractions when they are about to study, train them on how to remove them, such as internet access, television and mobile phones. Your students can set small goals and then reward themselves once they finish them. Keeping a diary or a planner is also very useful to write down notes and check for understanding and keep to deadlines and submission dates. Students with dyslexia can study with a study buddy or can borrow a study buddy's notes to ensure that they are following the flow of information.

Develop learners' executive functions

Executive functions are a group of higher cognitive abilities that control and regulate many functions and behaviours that are important to the learning process. Such abilities include working memory, attention, processing speed as well as inhibition and self-regulation. They are used to selectively process information in the environment and to retain task-relevant information in an accessible manner over time. Students with dyslexia demonstrate deficits in a variety of executive functions[31]. Compared to their typically achieving students, those with dyslexia show deficits in several executive functions such as verbal and phonological fluency, visual–spatial and auditory attention, verbal and visual short-term memory, and verbal working memory[32]. Executive functions are necessary for goal-directed behaviour, for the ability to initiate and stop actions, monitor and change behaviour when needed and for the ability to plan future behaviour when facing new tasks. Executive functions allow students with dyslexia to anticipate outcomes and adapt to changing situations[33].

Students with dyslexia use executive functions every day to learn, work and to manage their daily life. Trouble with their executive functions makes it hard for them to focus, follow directions and handle emotions. Such challenges cause students with dyslexia to have trouble starting and finishing their work. Their frustration also plays a role as their trouble with reading and writing can discourage them, making it hard to stay motivated. The more students with dyslexia use their executive functioning skills, the stronger they become as learners. Give them opportunities to practise focusing, thinking flexibly and keeping their information in mind. Encourage your students with dyslexia to reflect on their actions and responses to various questions and learning demands. Help them recognise the need for executive functions in their daily classroom activities such as pausing, considering their options and goals, and reflecting on their automatic reactions. Helping your students with dyslexia by breaking down assignments into smaller chunks and building in short breaks while working provides an aid to the deficits they experience in their executive functions which in turn boosts their motivation.

Notes

1 Shaffer et al., 2004.
2 www.crossboweducation.com.
3 'Funics' is produced by Ford & Tottman and is available from Crossbow Education.
4 www.smartkids.co.uk.
5 Berninger et al., 2002.
6 Bradley, 1990.
7 Stone, 2014.
8 Howlett, 2001.
9 Quirk & Schwanenflugel, 2004.

10 Fuchs et al., 1999.
11 Koskinen & Blum, 1986.
12 Topping, 1995.
13 https://en.wikipedia.org/wiki/Pomodoro_Technique.
14 Milani et al., 2010.
15 Gough & Tunmer, 1986.
16 Draffan et al., 2007.
17 Ferguson, 2007.
18 Wigfield & Guthrie, 1995.
19 Oka & Paris, 1987.
20 Desforges & Abouchaar, 2003.
21 Gonzalez-DeHass et al., 2005.
22 Grolnick et al., 1991.
23 www.structuredprocrastination.com/light.php.
24 Bruster, 2015.
25 International Dyslexia Association, dyslexiaida.org/multisensory-structured-language-teaching-fact-sheet.
26 Ehri, 2007.
27 Laishley et al., 2014.
28 Strickland et al., 2002.
29 www.skillsyouneed.com/learn/study-skills.
30 Mortimore & Crozier, 2006.
31 Reiter et al., 2004.
32 Varvara et al., 2014.
33 Smith-Spark et al., 2016.

Bibliography

Adams, K. & Christenson, S. (2000). Trust and the family-school relationship: Examination of parent-teacher differences in elementary and secondary grades. *Journal of School Psychology*, 38(5), 477–497.

Alan, B. & Fryer, R. (2011) Power and pitfalls of education incentives. A discussion paper published by the Hamilton Project and retrieved from their website: www.hamiltonproject.org in May 2020.

American Psychiatric Association (2013). *Diagnostic and statistical manual of mental disorders, 5th edition.* Arlington, VA: American Psychiatric Association.

Ames, C. (1992). Classrooms: Goals, structure and student motivation. *Journal of Educational Psychology*, 84(3), 261–271.

Baines, E., Blatchford, P. & Kutnick, P. (2003). Changes in grouping practices over primary and secondary school. *International Journal of Educational Research*, 39, 9–34.

Barry, N. (2007). Motivating the reluctant student. *American Music Teacher*, 56(5), 23–27.

Begg, I.M., Anas, A. & Farinacci, S. (1992) Dissociation of processes in belief: Source recollection, statement familiarity, and the illusion of truth. *Journal of Experimental Psychology: General*, 121(4), 446–458.

Berninger, V., Vaughan, K., Abbott, R., Begay, K., Coleman, K., Curtin, G. & Hawkins, J. (2002). Teaching spelling and composition alone and together: Implications for the Simple View of Writing, *Journal of Educational Psychology*, 94(2), 291–304.

Bradley, L. (1990). Rhyming connections in learning to read and spell. In P.D. Pumfrey & C.D. Elliott (Eds.), *Children's difficulties in reading, spelling and writing.* Abingdon, UK: Routledge.

Breen, R. & Lindsay, R. (2002). Different disciplines require different motivations for student success. *Research in Higher Education*, 43(6), 693–725.

Brewer, E. & Burgess, D. (2005). Professor's role in motivating students to attend class. *Journal of Industrial Teaching Education*, 42(23), 23–47.

Brewer, E., Dejong, J. & Stout, V. (2001). *Moving to online: Make the transition from traditional instruction and communication strategies.* Newbury Park, CA: Corwin Press.

Britt, T. (2005). The effects of identity-relevance and task difficulty on task motivation, stress, and performance. *Motivation and Emotion*, 29, 189–202.

Brophy, J. (1988). Research linking teacher behavior to student achievement: Potential implications for instruction of Chapter 1 students. *Educational Psychologist*, 23(3), 235–286.

Broussard, S. & Garrison, M. (2004). The relationship between classroom motivation and academic achievement in elementary school-aged children. *Family and Consumer Sciences Research Journal*, 33(2), 106–120.

Bruster, D.B. (2015). Poetry and writing: Improving fluency and motivation for students with developmental dyslexic traits. *Reading Improvement*, 52, 93–99.

Burton, S. (2004). Self-esteem groups for secondary pupils with dyslexia. *Educational Psychology in Practice*, 20(1), 55–73.

Butler, R. (1988) Enhancing and undermining intrinsic motivation: The effects of task-involving and ego-involving evaluation of interest and performance. *British Journal of Educational Psychology*, 58(1), 1–14.

Chan, L.K.S. (1994). Relationship of motivation, strategic learning, and reading achievement in Grades 5, 7, and 9. *Journal of Experimental Education*, 62(4), 319–339.

Clifford, M.M. (1972) Effects of competition as a motivational technique in the classroom. *American Educational Research Journal*, 9, 123–137.

Cooper, H. & Lindsay, J. (2000). Homework in the home: How student, family, and parenting-style differences relate to the homework process. *Contemporary Educational Psychology*, 25(4), 464–487.

Cooper, H., Lindsay, J., Nye, B. & Greathouse, S. (1998). Relationships among attitudes about homework, amount of homework assigned and completed and student achievement. *Journal of Educational Psychology*, 90(1), 70–83.

Covington, M.V. (2002). Rewards and intrinsic motivation: A needs-based developmental perspective. In F. Pajares & T. Urdan (Eds.), *Academic motivation of adolescents.* Greenwich, CT: Information Age Publishing, 1–27.

Crossbow Education: www.crossboweducation.com Accessed 17 May 2020.

Csikszentmihalyi, M. (2009). *Flow.* Harper-Collins, e-books.

Davis, B. (1999). *Motivating students.* University of California, Berkley: Jossey-Bass.

Deci, E. & Ryan, R. (1985). *Intrinsic motivation and self-determination in human behaviour.* New York: Plenum.

Desforges, C. & Abouchaar, A. (2003). *The impact of parental involvement, parental support and family education on pupil achievements and adjustment: A literature review.* London: DfES Publications.

Diigo: www.diigo.com/ Accessed on 23 May 2020.

Dörnyei, Z. (2001). *Motivational strategies in the language classroom.* Cambridge, England: Cambridge University Press.

Dörnyei, Z. (2003). Attitudes, orientation, and motivations in language learning: Advances in theory, research, and applications. *Language Learning*, 53, 3–32.

Dörnyei, Z. (2011) *Teaching and researching motivation.* Harlow: Longman. E-learning.

Dörnyei, Z. & Ushioda, E. (2013) *Teaching and researching motivation.* New York: Routledge.

Draffan, E.A., Evans, D.G. & Blenkhorn, P. (2007). Use of assistive technology by students with dyslexia in post-secondary education. *Disability & Rehabilitation: Assistive Technology*, 2(2), 105–116.

Dunlap, G., Kern-Dunlap, L., Clarke, S. & Robbins, G.R. (1991). Functional assessment, curricular revision, and severe behavior problems. *Journal of Applied Behaviour Analysis*, 24, 387–397.

Eccles, J. & Wigfield, A. (2002). Motivational beliefs, values and goals. *Annual Review of Psychology*, 53(1), 109–132.

Education Development Trust (2016). Report by the Education Development Trust. Obtained from their website: www.educationdevelopmenttrust.com in May 2020.

Ehri, L.C. (2007). Development of sight word reading: Phases and findings. In M.J. Snowling & C. Hulme (Eds.), *The science of reading: A handbook.* Oxford: Blackwell.

Elikai, F. & Schuhmann, P. (2010). An examination of the impact of grading policies on students' achievements. *Issues in Accounting Education*, 25(4), 677–693.

Elliot, E.S. & Dweck, C.S. (1988). Goals: An approach to motivation and achievement. *Journal of Personality and Social Psychology*, 54, 5–12.

Ferguson, R. (2007). Research based tips for high achievement parenting. Retrieved from: http://groundcontrolparenting.wordpress.com/2011/03/05/dr-ronald-ferguson-what-parents-can-do/

Fuchs, L., Fuchs, D. & Kazdan, S. (1999). Effects of peer-assisted learning strategies on high school students with serious reading problems. *Remedial and Special Education*, 20(5), 309–318.

Gest, S.D. & Rodkin, P.C. (2011). Teaching practices and elementary classroom peer ecologies. *Journal of Applied Developmental Psychology*, 32, 288–296.

Gonzalez-DeHass, A., Willems, P. & Holbein, M. (2005). Examining the relationship between parental involvement and student motivation. *Educational Psychology Review*, 17(2), 99–123.

Goodreads: www.goodreads.com Accessed on 12 May 2020.

Gottfried, A. (2009). Commentary: The role of environment in contextual and social influences on motivation: Generalities, specifics and causality. In K. Wentzel & A. Wigfield (Eds.), *Handbook of Motivation at School*. New York: Routledge.

Gottfried, A.E., Fleming, J.S. & Gottfried, A.W. (2001). Continuity of academic intrinsic motivation from childhood through late adolescence: A longitudinal study. *Journal of Educational Psychology*, 93(1), 3–13.

Gough, P.B. & Tunmer, W.E. (1986). Decoding, reading, and reading disability. *Remedial and Special Education*, 7(1), 6–10.

Graham, S. & Weiner, B. (1996) Theories and principles of motivation. In D.C. Berliner & R.C. Calfee (Eds.), *Handbook of educational psychology*. New York: Simon & Schuster Macmillan.

Grolnick, W., Ryan, R. & Deci, E. (1991) Inner resources for school achievement: Motivational mediators of children's perceptions of their parents. *Journal of Educational Psychology*, 83(4), 508–517.

Guay, F., Chanal, J., Ratelle, C., Marsh, H., Larose, S. & Boivin, M. (2010) Intrinsic, identified and controlled types of motivation for school subjects in young elementary school children. *British Journal of Educational Psychology*. 80(4), 711–735.

Guthrie, J., Wigfield, A. & VonSecker, C. (2000). Effects of integrated instruction on motivation and strategy use in reading. *Journal of Educational Psychology*, 92(2), 331–341.

Hamilton, L., Halverson, R., Jackson, S., Mandinach, E., Supovitz, J. & Wayman, J. (2009). *Using student achievement data to support instructional decision making (NCEE 2009–4067)*. Washington, DC: National Center for Education Evaluation and Regional Assistance, Institute of Education Sciences, U.S. Department of Education.

Hamm, J. & Faircloth, B. (2005). The role of friendship in adolescents' sense of school belonging. *New Directions for Child and Adolescent Development*, 2005(107), 61–78.

Hamre, B. & Pianta, R. (2001). Early teacher–child relationships and the trajectory of children's school outcomes through eighth grade. *Child Development*, 72(2), 625–638.

Hancock, D. (2002). Influencing postsecondary students' motivation to learn in the classroom. *College Teaching*, 50(2), 63–66.

Harkin, B., Webb, T.L., Chang, B.P.I., Prestwich, A., Conner, M., Kellar, I., Benn, Y. & Sheeran, P. (2016). Does monitoring goal progress promote goal attainment? A meta-analysis of the experimental evidence. *Psychological Bulletin*, 142(2), 198–229.

Harvey E. & Kenyon M. (2013). Classroom seating considerations for 21st century students and faculty. *Journal of Learning Spaces*, 2(1).

Hasher, l., Goldstein, D. & Toppino, T. (1977) Frequency and the conference of referential validity. *Journal of verbal learning and verbal behaviour*, 16, 107–112.

Hattie, J. & Timperley, H. (2007). The power of feedback. *Review of Educational Research*, 77(1), 81–112.

Hidi, S. & Harackiewicz, J. (2000). Motivating the academically unmotivated: A critical issue for the 21st century. *Review of Educational Research*, 70(2), 151–179.

Hom Jr., H.L. & Maxwell, F.R. (1983). The impact of task difficulty expectations on intrinsic motivation. *Motivation and Emotion*, 7, 19–24.

Howlett, C. (2001). Dyslexia and biology. In L. Peer & G. Reid (Eds.), *Dyslexia: Successful inclusion in the secondary school*. London: David Fulton.

Huitt, W. (2011). Motivation to learn: An overview. *Educational Psychology Interactive*. Valdosta, GA: Valdosta State University.

Inspiring Teachers; How teachers inspire learners, 2016: www.education developmenttrust.com/our-research-and-insights/research/inspiring-teachers-how-teachers-inspire-learners Accessed 12 May 2020.

International Dyslexia Association: https://dyslexiaida.org/multisensory-structured-language-teaching-fact-sheet/ Accessed on 10 June 2020.

Kern, L. & Clemens, N.H. (2007). Antecedent strategies to promote appropriate classroom behaviour. *Psychology in the Schools*, 44(1), 65–75.

Koskinen, P. & Blum, I. (1986). Paired repeated reading: A classroom strategy for developing fluent reading. *The Reading Teacher*, 40(1), 70–75.

Laishley, A., Liversedge, S. & Kirkby, J. (2014). Lexical processing in children and adults during word copying. *Journal of Cognitive Psychology*, 27(5), 1–16.

Lepper, M. & Chabay, R. (1985). Intrinsic motivation and instruction: Conflicting views on the role of motivational processes in computer-based education. *Educational Psychologist*, 20(4), 217–230.

Li, W., Lee, A. & Solmon, M. (2007). The role of perceptions of task difficulty in relation to self-perceptions of ability, intrinsic value, attainment value, and performance. *European Physical Education Review*, 13, 301–312.

Lifehacker. Productivity 101: An introduction to the Pomodoro Technique: https://lifehacker.com/productivity-101-a-primer-to-the-pomodoro-technique-1598992730 Accessed on 26 May 2020.

Linnenbrink, E. & Pintrich, P. (2003). The role of self-efficacy beliefs in student engagement and learning in the classroom. *Reading & Writing Quarterly*, 19(2), 119–137.

Linnenbrink-Garcia, L., Tyson, D.F. & Patall, E.A. (2008). When are achievement goal orientations beneficial for academic achievement? A closer look at moderating factors. *International Review of Social Psychology*, 21(1), 19–70.

Locke, E. & Latham, G. (2002). Building a practically useful theory of goal setting and task motivation. *American Psychologist*, 57, 705–717.

Maehr, M.L. & Zusho, A. (2009). Achievement goal theory: The past, present, and future. In K.R. Wentzel & A. Wigfield (Eds.), *Handbook of Motivation at School*. New York: Routledge.

Margolis, H. & McCabe, P.P. (2004) Self-efficacy: A key to improving the motivation of struggling learners. *The Clearing House*, 77(6), 241–249.

Marsh, H. & Kleitman, S. (2003) School athletic participation: Mostly gain with little pain. *Journal of Sport and Exercise Psychology*, 25(2), 205–228.

Martin, A. (2009). Motivation and engagement across the academic life span: A developmental construct validity study of elementary school, high school and university/college students. *Educational and Psychological Measurement*, 69(5), 794–824.

Maslow, A.H. (1943). *Motivation and personality*. New York: Harper.

Maynard, D.C. & Hakel, M.D. (1997). Effects of objective and subjective task complexity on task performance. *Human Performance*, 10, 303–330.

McClelland, D. (2001). Achievement motivation. In W.E. Natemeyer & J.T. McMahon (Eds.) *Classics of organizational behavior*, 3rd Edition. Long Grove, IL: Waveland Press.

McKeown, S., Stringer, M. & Cairns, E. (2015). Classroom segregation: Where do students sit and how is this related to group relations? *British Educational Research Journal*, 42(1), 40–55.

McLean, A. (2004). *The motivated school*. London: Sage.

Melnick, M. & Sabo, D. (1992). Educational effects of interscholastic athletic participation on African American and Hispanic youth. *Adolescence*, 27(106), 295–308.

Milani, A., Lorusso, M.L. & Molteni, M. (2010). The effects of audio-books on the psychosocial adjustment of pre-adolescents and adolescents with dyslexia. *Dyslexia*, 16(1), 87–97.

Mo, J. (2019). How is students' motivation related to their performance and anxiety? *PISA in Focus, No. 92*, Paris: OECD Publishing. www.oecd-ilibrary.org/docserver/d7c28431-en.pdf Accessed on 17 May 2020.

Mortimore, T. & Crozier, W. (2006): Dyslexia and difficulties with study skills in higher education. *Studies in Higher Education*, 31(2), 235–251.

NASA: www.grc.nasa.gov/WWW/K-12/airplane/newton1g.html#:~:text=His%20first%20law%20states%20that,action%20of%20an%20external%20force. Accessed on 22 June 2020.

National Research Council. (2004). *Engaging schools: Fostering high school students' motivation to learn*. Washington, DC: The National Academies Press.

O'Connor, E. & McCartney, K. (2007). Examining teacher-child relationships and achievement as part of an ecological model of development. *American Educational Research Journal*, 44(2), 340–369.

OECD: www.oecd.org Accessed on 17 May 2020

Oka, E.R. & Paris, S.G. (1987). Patterns of motivation and reading skills in under-achieving children. In S.J. Ceci (Ed.), *Handbook of cognitive, social and neurological aspects of learning disabilities*, Vol II. Hillsdale, NJ: LEA.

Osterman, K. (2000). Students' need for belonging in the school community. *Review of Educational Research*, 70(3), 323–367.

Pachran, P., Bay, D. & Felton, S. (2013). The impact of a flexible assessment system on students' motivation, performance and attitude. *Accounting Education: An International Journal*, 22(12), 147–167.

Park, L. & Crocker, J. (2013). Pursuing self-esteem: Implications for self-regulation and relationships. In V. Zeigler-Hill (Ed.), *Self-esteem* (pp. 43–59). New York, NY: Psychology Press.

PassItOn: www.passiton.com/inspirational-quotes Accessed on 12 May 2020.

Pintirch, P. (2003). A motivational science perspective on the role of student motivation in learning and teaching contexts. *Journal of Educational Psychology*, 95(4), 667–686.

Pintrich, P. & DeGroot, E. (1990). Motivational and self-regulated learning components of classroom academic performance. *Journal of Educational Psychology*, 82(1), 33–40.

Pomodoro Technique: https://en.wikipedia.org/wiki/Pomodoro_Technique Accessed on 7 June 2020.

Quirk, M. & Schwanenflugel, P. (2004). Do supplemental remedial reading programs address the motivational issues of struggling readers? An analysis of five popular programs. *Reading Research and Instruction*, 43(1), 1–19.

Rands, M. & Gansemer-Topf A. (2017). The room itself is active: How classroom design impacts student engagement. *Journal of Learning Spaces*, 6(1).

Ratey, N. & Sleeper-Triplett, J. (2011). Strategic coaching for LD and ADHD. In S. Goldstein, J. Naglieri & M. DeVries (Eds.), *Learning and attention disorders in adolescence and adulthood: Assessment and treatment*. New York: Wiley.

Reiter, A., Tucha, O. & Lange, K. (2004). Executive functions in children with dyslexia. *Dyslexia, An international Journal of Research & Practice*, 11(2) 116–131.

Riddick, B., Sterling, C., Farmer, M. & Morgan, S. (1999) Self-esteem and anxiety in the educational histories of adult dyslexic students. *Dyslexia: An International Journal of Research and Practice*, 5(4), 227–248.

Rigby, C., Deci, E., Patrick, B. & Ryan, R. (1992). Beyond the intrinsic-extrinsic dichotomy: Self-determination in motivation and learning. *Motivation and Emotion*, 16(3), 165–185.

Roe, B., Smith, S. & Burns, P. (2005). *Teaching reading in today's elementary school*. Boston: Houghton Mifflin Company.

Ryan, R. & Deci, E. (2000a). Intrinsic and extrinsic motivation: Classic definitions and new directions. *Contemporary Educational Psychology*. 25, 54–67.

Ryan, R. & Deci, E. (2000b). The 'What' and 'Why' of goal pursuits: Human needs and the self-determination of behaviour. *Psychological Inquiry*, 11(4), 227–268.

Ryan, A.M., Kuusinen, C.M. & Bedoya-Skoog, A. (2015). Managing peer relations: A dimension of teacher self-efficacy that varies between elementary and middle school teachers and is associated with observed classroom quality. *Contemporary Educational Psychology*, 41, 147–156.

ScholarChip: https://scholarchip.com/incentive-for-students Accessed on 13 May 2020.

Schuitema, J., Peetsma, T. & van der Veen, I. (2012). Self-regulated learning and students' perceptions of innovative and traditional learning environments: A longitudinal study in secondary education. *Educational Studies*, 38(4), 397–413.

Scott, T., Anderson, C. & Alter, P. (2012). *Managing classroom behavior using positive behaviour supports*. Upper Saddle River, NJ: Pearson Education, Inc.

Sencibaugh, J.M. & Sencibaugh, A.M. (2016). An analysis of cooperative learning approaches for students with learning disabilities. *Education*, 136(3), 356–364.

Shaffer, D., Squire, K., Halverson, R. & Gee, J. (2004). *Video games and the future of learning*. Madison, WI: University of Wisconson-Madison & Academic Advanced Distributed Learning Co-Laboratory.

Shaklee, H. (1976). Development in inferences of ability and task difficulty. *Child Development*, 47, 1051–1057.

Shimabukuro, S., Prater, M., Jenkins, A. & Edelen-Smith, P. (1999). The effects of self-monitoring of academic performance on students with learning disabilities and ADD/ADHD. *Education and Treatment of Children*, 22(4), 397–414.

Shulruf, B. (2010). Do extra-curricular activities in schools improve educational outcomes? A critical review and meta-analysis of the literature. *International Review of Education*, 56(5–6), 591–612.

Skills You Need: www.skillsyouneed.com/learn/study-skills.html Accessed 17 June 2020.

Smartkids: www.smarkids.com Accessed 17 May 2020.

Smith-Spark, J., Henry, L., Messer, D., Edvardsdottir, E. & Zięcik, A. (2016). Executive functions in adults with developmental dyslexia. *Research in Developmental Disabilities*, 56, 197–203.

Smythe, I., Everatt, J. & Salter, R. (Eds.). (2004). *The international book of dyslexia: A cross-language comparison and practice guide* (Second ed.). Chichester: Wiley & Sons.

Spence, I., Wong, P., Rusan, M. & Rastegar, N. (2006): How colour enhances visual memory for natural scenes. *Psychological Science*, 17(1), 1–6.

Stipek, D. (1996) Motivation and instruction. In D.C. Berliner & R.C. Calfee (Eds.), *Handbook of Educational Psychology* (pp. 85–113). New York: Macmillan.

Stipek, D. (2002). *Motivation to learn: Integrating theory and practice*. Massachusetts: Allyn and Bacon.

Stipek, D., Feiler, R., Daniels, D. & Milburn, S. (1995) Effects of different instructional approaches on young children's achievement and motivation. *Child Development*, 66(1), 209–223.

Stone, L. (2014). *Spelling for life: Uncovering the simplicity and science of spelling*. London: Routledge.

Strickland, D.S., Ganske, K. & Monroe, J.K. (2002). *Supporting struggling readers and writers: Strategies for classroom intervention 3–6*. Newark, DE: International Reading Association.

Structured Procrastination: www.structuredprocrastination.com/light.php Accessed on 10 June 2020.

Tao Te Ching – Lao Tzu – A Comparative Study: www.wussu.com/laotzu/laotzu64.html Accessed on 13 May 2020.

The British Dyslexia Association: www.bdadyslexia.org.uk/dyslexia/about-dyslexia/what-is-dyslexia Accessed 26 May 2020.

The International Classifications of Diseases: https://icd.codes/icd10cm/F810 Accessed 26 May 2020.

The International Dyslexia Association: https://dyslexiaida.org/definition-of-dyslexia/ Accessed 26 May 2020.

The physics classroom: www.physicsclassroom.com/class/newtlaws/Lesson-3/Newton-s-Second-Law# Accessed on 22 June 2020.

Topping, K. (1995). *Paired reading, spelling and writing: The handbook for teachers and parents*. London: Continuum International Publishing Group.

Trussell, R.P. (2008). Classroom universals to prevent problem behaviours. *Intervention in School and Clinic*, 43, 179–185.

Turner, J. (1995). The influence of classroom contexts on young children's motivation for literacy. *Reading Research Quarterly*, 30(3), 410–441.

Understanding Anxiety in Children & Teens: 2018 Children's Mental Health Report. Child Mind Institute: https://childmind.org/downloads/CMI_2018CMHR.pdf Accessed on 16 May 2020.

Usher, A. & Kober, N. (2012). *Student motivation: An overlooked piece of school reform*. Washington: Centre on Educational Policy, George Washington University.

Van den Berg, Y., Segers, E. & Cillessen, A. (2012). Changing peer perceptions and victimization through classroom arrangements: A field experiment. *Journal Abnormal Child Psychology*, 40, 403–412.

Varvara, P., Varuzza, C., Sorrentino, A., Vicari, S. & Menghini, D. (2014). Executive functions in developmental dyslexia. *Frontiers in Human Neuroscience*, 8, 120.

Vroom, V.H. (1964). *Work and motivation*. Wiley.

Vygotsky, L. (1978). *Mind in society: The development of higher psychological processes*. Cambridge, MA: Harvard University Press.

Wayman, J.C. (2005). Involving teachers in data-driven decision-making: Using computer data systems to support teacher inquiry and reflection. *Journal of Education for Students Placed at Risk*, 10(3), 295–308.

Webb, N. (1989). Peer interaction and learning in small groups. *Journal of Educational Research*, 13, 21–39.

Weiner, B. (1979). A theory of motivation for some classroom experiences. *Journal of Educational Psychology*, 71, 3–25.

Wentzel, K. (1997). Student motivation in middle school: The role of perceived pedagogical caring. *Journal of Educational Psychology*, 89(3), 411–419.

Whoosreading: www.whooosreading.org/ Accessed on 23 May 2020.

Wigfield, A. & Guthrie, J. T. (1995). *Dimensions of children's motivation for reading: An initial study*. Athens, GA: National Reading Research Centre.

Willingham, D. (2008). Should learning be its own reward? *American Educator*, 31(4), 29–35.

Wilson, J. (2011). Students' perspective on intrinsic motivation to learn: A model to guide educators. *International Christian Community for Teacher Education Journal*, 6(1).

Wilson, K. & Boldeman, S. (2012). Exploring ICT integration as a tool to engage young people at a flexible learning centre. *Journal of Science Education & Technology*, 21(6), 661–668.

Wohlstetter, P., Datnow, A. & Park, V. (2008). Creating a system for data-driven decision-making: Applying the principal-agent framework. *School Effectiveness and School Improvement*, 19(3), 239–259.

Wray, D. (1994). *Literacy and Awareness*. London: Hodder & Stoughton.

Index

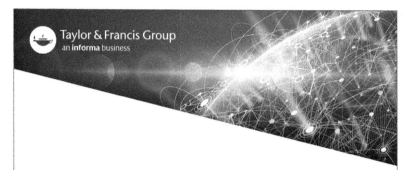